A Student's Guide to ITALIAN AMERICAN Genealogy

Oryx American Family Tree Series

A Student's Guide to ITALIAN AMERICAN Genealogy

By Terra Castiglia Brockman

 Oryx Press
1996

For my Italian grandparents, Saveria Novello Castiglia and Pasquale Castiglia, who came to America to start new lives and through hard work and heartache raised five Italian American children, Joseph, Virginia, Attilio, Lena, and my mother, Marlene Castiglia Brockman, whose many talents and unfailing love have given her six children a priceless heritage.

Copyright 1996 by The Rosen Publishing Group, Inc.
Published in 1996 by The Oryx Press
4041 North Central at Indian School Road
Phoenix, Arizona 85012-3397

Printed and bound in the United States of America

Library of Congress Cataloging-in-Publication Data
Brockman, Terra Castiglia
    A student's guide to Italian American genealogy/Terra Castiglia Brockman.
        p.   cm.—(The Oryx American family tree)
    Includes bibliographical references and index.
    ISBN 0-89774-973-1 (alk. paper)
    1. Italian Americans—Genealogy—Handbooks, manuals, etc.
    2. Italian Americans—Genealogy—Bibliography.
I. Title. II. Series: Oryx American family tree.
E184.I8886   1996   95-47314
929'.1'08951073—dc20   CIP

Contents

Chapter 1
Why Trace Your Roots?

"Know thyself," it is inscribed in the Temple of Apollo at Delphi. It is an idea that has echoed through the ages. In *Hamlet*, the English playwright Shakespeare wrote, "To thine own self be true." The Spanish novelist Cervantes wrote, "Make it thy business to know thyself." And the Italian poet Dante wrote, "Consider your origin."

All these people wrote of the value of self-knowledge. With a clear sense of who you are, you can be more confident of your thoughts, feelings, and actions. One way to learn more about yourself is through genealogy, the study of your family's heritage. Genealogy helps you to know more about two kinds of heritage. The first is your genetic heritage, the qualities you inherited from your biological relatives. The second is your cultural heritage, the customs and ways of thinking, speaking, and acting that came from the family and larger community you grew up in.

Discovering Your Genetic Heritage

Your genetic, or biological, heritage consists of the traits that were passed on to you from your ancestors. You may have the dimples and quiet demeanor of your father, the thin body and high energy of your grandmother, or the deep brown eyes and relaxed disposition of your Uncle Joe. As you learn about your ancestors' lives, you may discover something about your own life—present, past, and future. For example, if there are many athletes, artists, or musicians in your family, it is likely that you will have some of these same talents.

Your genetic heritage is the result of a unique mingling of genetic material. It can be compared to a random hand of

The author's Italian American mother, aunts, and grandmother (left to right) pose outside a Chicago church in the early 1950s. Your own research will allow you to affirm your family's connection to Italy and the immigrant experience.

cards that is dealt in a card game. Your hand of cards was determined the moment you were conceived and will remain with you throughout your life. How you play your cards has much to do with the environment, the particular physical and social setting you live in. Although you cannot change your genetic heritage, you will have opportunities to change your environment as you grow older.

The environment that your family members lived in strongly influenced their personalities and outlook on life. Imagine the personality of a person who is brought up surrounded by friends and family in a large house in a pleasant city, where there is always plenty of love, laughter, music, and good food. Now imagine that same person brought up in a tiny, isolated village in a harsh environment where there is hard labor every day from sunrise to sunset and seldom enough to eat. After a lifetime in the first environment, a person may be happy-go-lucky, generous, and open. A lifetime in the second might produce a bitter, resentful, unfriendly person. On the other hand, the first environment might produce a fat, lazy, unhappy person, while the second could produce a hard-working, productive, cheerful person. It all depends on the person's particular set of inherited characteristics and the way they interact with a particular environment. When you find out more about what made your ancestors the kind of people they were, you will begin to gain insights into what has made you the kind of person you are. You may also catch glimpses of the person you could become in the future.

Celebrating Your Cultural Heritage

Your cultural heritage may have little or nothing to do with your genetic heritage. If you were adopted or live in a nontraditional family, your genealogical search may have much more to do with learning about your cultural heritage. You may not have a single biological link to an Italian or Italian American, but if you grew up around people who do, researching their family trees will tell you a great deal about them. As you find out more about these people and their ancestors, you will better understand the impact this heritage has had on you.

Cultural heritage can have such an enormous impact on a person's life that you may want to use some of the techniques described in this book to explore the cultural heritage of a person who is neither a relative nor a member of your adoptive family or community. Perhaps you'd like to look into the impact of Italian cultural heritage on, for example, the film director Francis Ford Coppola, the actor Robert DeNiro, or the first female vice-presidential candidate, Geraldine Ferraro. Such research would add depth and interest to a minibiography or report on the person.

No matter whether you live with two biological parents or one, a grandparent or more distant relative, or adoptive parents, you can still engage in meaningful genealogical research. Researching the family tree of one or two biological parents will give you insight into your genetic and cultural heritage. Concentrating on one biological parent or relative allows you to go back even more generations than if you were researching both sides of a family tree. Researching your adoptive parents' family tree will give you a greater understanding of how their cultural heritage has influenced you. No matter what your particular family is like, genealogical research can be challenging and rewarding.

Learning History and Geography through Genealogy

Genealogy is a way to learn not only about yourself and your family, but also about how your family has been affected by larger historical events. Genealogical research is intimately connected with history, geography, politics, and economics. Most Italians who came to the United States were driven by economic hardship—dire poverty in "the old country." Here is how one Sicilian immigrant remembers it:

> It was unbearable. My brother Luigi was six then and I was seven. Every morning we'd get up before sunrise and start walking about four or five miles to the farm of the *patrunu*—the boss. Many times we went without breakfast. For lunch we ate a piece of bread and plenty of water. If we were lucky, sometimes we would have a small piece of cheese or an onion. We worked in the hot sun until the late afternoon, then we had to drag ourselves home . . . so tired we could barely eat, and fell asleep with all our clothes on . . . And life went on this way day in and day out.[1]

Why did such young boys have to work so hard? Why were they hungry? Why was Italy in poverty? Did these kinds of conditions occur only in this part of Italy? What led so many people to leave the villages where they were born and from which they had never before ventured? Why did people go to America, rather than to neighboring countries in Europe? The answers to these questions come from history.

---

[1] Mangione, Jerre, and Morreale, Ben. *La Storia: Five Centuries of the Italian American Experience* (New York: HarperCollins, 1992).

Italian and Italian American culture is famous for its emphasis on family and tradition. Family ties are strong.

History, in turn, is influenced by geography, politics, and economics.

In searching for your roots you'll come to a personal understanding of historical forces and how they affected your family. You will begin to discover this history from your own relatives and from their friends and relatives. Gradually, you will be able to attach family names to historical events, places, and dates. Then you will flesh out this historical skeleton with the personalities and accomplishments of your ancestors. At the same time, you will learn more about history and geography, as well as about politics and economics and perhaps even science, literature, and philosophy.

From Columbus to Colombo: An Overview

Italians and Italian Americans have played a crucial role in the history of the United States. From the name "America," to the writing of the Declaration of Independence, to the founding of the Bank of America, to the films of Francis Ford Coppola, to the aromas of pasta and pizza—these are just a few of the contributions to American culture made by Italians and Italian Americans.

The first encounter between Italy and the United States happened long before either was a nation. In 1492 Cristoforo Colombo, the man we call Christopher Columbus, sailed to the land we now call the United States of America. We call it America after another Italian, Amerigo Vespucci, who in 1502 declared that the new land was not part of the East Indies, but "a New World."

The first Italian immigrant to the Americas, Peter Caesar Alberti, came with the Dutch in 1635 and raised his family on what is now Long Island in New York State. Italian immigration was rare during the colonial period of the seventeenth and eighteenth centuries. The few Italians living in the United States by the early nineteenth century were mostly artisans, stonecutters, sculptors, and painters from northern Italy.

It was not until the 1870s and 1880s that Italians began to arrive in significant numbers. From 1870 to 1920, more than four million Italians came to the United States. They settled mainly in the industrial cities of the Northeast and Midwest: New York, Boston, Philadelphia, and Chicago. Some also settled in the rural deep South, as well as in California, where the climate resembled that of their homeland.

The vast majority of these immigrants were peasants from the overpopulated, impoverished regions of southern Italy, especially Calabria and Sicily. Seeking better economic opportunities, the immigrants left their sunny fishing villages on the Mediterranean and their tiny farming communities in the interior mountains and crossed the Atlantic to the United States. Some continued their agrarian pursuits, selling fruits and vegetables or planting grapevines brought from Italy and establishing wineries. Most, however, began a new life—working in the factories of northern industrial

Italian émigrés and their descendants have risen to the top of their fields in many professions. The Nobel Prize-winning physicist Enrico Fermi is shown here during a lecture in 1949.

cities, the railroad construction sites in the Midwest and West, the iron mines of Minnesota, and the copper and silver mines of California. At first these laborers were called "birds of passage" because they came and went seasonally, working in the United States as long as the weather was good, then returning to their families in Italy for the winter months. Some remained "birds of passage," but most ended up bringing their wives and children and staying in the United States.

Today the descendants of these Italian immigrants number in the millions and live throughout the United States. They participate in every facet of American society, from cattle-ranching in Montana to bread-baking in Providence. In universities, corporations, city halls, sports arenas,

theaters, state legislatures, Congress, and the Supreme
Court, one can find descendants of Italian immigrants. You
will find accomplished Italian Americans in virtually every
profession in the United States—and some of them may be
part of your family tree.

Starting Your Genealogical Journey

When I asked my mother why her parents had come to
Chicago from their small village in southern Italy, her answer was simple: In Italy, there was nothing to eat. My
grandmother had told her that the earth was as hard and dry
as rock. People would scrape at it with picks and shovels and
try to plant vegetables. But without rain, there was no food.
When the villagers began to hear rumors of the jobs and
wealth to be found in North and South America, their
minds were made up. My grandmother's entire village,
except for the elderly, left to start new lives in the United
States and in Argentina.

In southern Italy, this was not uncommon. From 1870
until 1914, over one-third of the inhabitants of southern
Italy emigrated. In 1901, the mayor of the southern Italian
town of Moliterno met Italy's prime minister with the words:
"I greet you in the name of eight thousand fellow citizens,
three thousand of whom are in America and the other five
thousand preparing to follow them."

The reason his townspeople and so many others emigrated
appeared simple—they were slowly starving. But there were
many complex reasons beneath this simple one. The people
of the south were starving because a feudal system gave over
large tracts of land to a single owner. Peasants worked the
land all day for a small portion of the produce, hardly
enough to keep them alive. On top of this man-made hardship were natural problems such as drought and disease.

From the age of eighteen until her death at the age of
eighty-nine, my grandmother never returned to Italy and
never saw her own mother again. None of us took the time
to record her story or her memories of her family. When she
died, these memories were lost.

If you have even the slightest interest in your family history, the time to start is now, before your most precious and irreplaceable resources—your own elderly relatives and their treasure trove of memories—are lost. This is the best place to start to find out more about your family members and the forces that made them who they are—and made you who you are.

As you pursue your family history, be respectful toward your relatives and their friends. Most people will be more than willing to share their memories and experiences with you, but some, for personal reasons, may prefer not to. If this is the case, remember that everyone has a right to privacy. If someone is not willing to be interviewed, thank them and move on to the next person on your list or turn to sources in libraries and archives. Either way, the information you discover will be vital to understanding your family history.

Resources

STARTING YOUR EXPLORATION

Angelillo, Barbara Walsh. *Italy*. Austin, TX: Steck-Vaughn, 1991.

A look at Italy's history, its tradition of art and music, the importance of family, and historic sites. This book also covers industry, religion, education, and health in Italy.

DiFranco, J. P. *The Italian Americans*. New York: Chelsea House, 1995.

Information on Italian history and culture and the story of Italian emigration. Illustrated with photographs, maps, and graphics. Part of *The Immigrant Experience* series.

Sproule, Anna. *Italy*. Columbus, OH: Silver Burdett, 1987.

A lively, informative view of history, geography, and culture. Illustrated with color photographs, maps, diagrams, and charts.

Witkoski, M. *Italian Americans*. Vero Beach, FL: Rourke, 1992.

This book traces the history of Italian Americans, explaining why they came to the United States and where they settled. The book describes some of the Italian contributions to American culture through foods, festivals, and family traditions.

WHY TRACE YOUR ROOTS?

Alba, Richard D. *Italian Americans: Into the Twilight of Ethnicity*. Englewood, NJ: Prentice-Hall, 1985.

A short study of the social and cultural history of Italian immigrants in the United States and how their conditions have changed over time. Includes demographic information.

Allen, James Paul, and Turner, Eugene James. *We the People: An Atlas of America's Ethnic Diversity*. **New York: Macmillan, 1988.**

A comprehensive study, with maps and essays, of immigrant dispersion in the United States.

Barzini, Luigi. *The Italians*. **New York: McGraw-Hill, 1964.**

An overview of the history and national character of Italians.

Chermayeff, Ivan, et al. *Ellis Island: An Illustrated History of the Immigrant Experience*. **New York: Macmillan, 1991.**

A good introduction to the immigrant experience.

Davie, Maurice R. *World Immigration with Special Reference to the United States*. **New York: Macmillan, 1936. Reprinted by Garland, 1983.**

Gives statistics on all immigration, including the great wave of Italian immigration in the early part of the twentieth century.

Gallo, Patrick J. *Old Bread, New Wine: A Portrait of the Italian-Americans*. **Chicago: Nelson-Hall, 1981.**

This book tells the epic story of the Italian American experience, beginning with the cultural and political history of Italy and ending with the effects of the migration on the immigrants and their descendants.

Greenhill, Basil. *The Great Migration: Crossing the Atlantic Under Sail*. **New York: Hastings House Publishers, 1974.**

This book provides many illustrated descriptions of the accommodations in wooden sailing ships and early steamships.

LoGatto, the Reverend Anthony. *The Italians in America, 1492–1972.* **Dobbs Ferry, NY: Oceana Publications, 1972.**

A volume of chronology and data on Italian Americans.

Peskett, Hugh. *Discovering Your Ancestors: A Quest for Your Roots.* **New York: Arco Publishers, 1978.**

Before plunging into your search, you may want to first see what you're getting into. This book is an overview of the research process for beginning genealogists.

Tomasi, Silvano M., and Engel, Madeline H., eds. *The Italian Experience in the United States.* **Staten Island, NY: Center for Migration Studies, 1970.**

An overview of the experiences of Italians in the United States.

Wright, Norman E. *Preserving Your American Heritage.* **Provo, UT: Brigham Young University Press, 1981.**

A book to inspire you to begin researching your heritage. Includes useful information on genealogical procedures and sources.

Chapter 2
The History of Italian Immigration

Of the hundreds of nationalities and ethnic groups that have been woven into the American fabric, the Italian thread is one of the longest and strongest. For five hundred years—before the United States and Italy were nations—people from the peninsula that would become Italy had a great influence on the land that would become the United States. From the fifteenth to the eighteenth centuries, explorers and adventurers such as Amerigo Vespucci, Christopher Columbus, and Giovanni Caboto (John Cabot) arrived on North American shores in the service of the European powers of France, Spain, and England, respectively. In the nineteenth century, many highly accomplished and talented Italians came to the fledgling United States—artists, musicians, painters, sculptors, writers, and philosophers.

Then, at the turn of the twentieth century, millions of Italians left their newly unified nation for a better life in the United States. The masses of poor, unskilled laborers from rural southern Italy and Sicily became the anonymous urban workforce that built railroads, tunnels, and skyscrapers and worked in factories and farms in cities and towns across the nation. In a few decades, they also became well-known figures in science, sports, music, politics, and films.

A Brief History of Italy

The Italian American experience is far more than pizza and pasta. The story begins in Italy, a land with an ancient history. Italy was influenced over millennia by people of many ethnicities: the Etruscans, Greeks, Romans, Byzantines, Saracens, Normans, French, and Spanish. The Etruscans, who lived in and around Tuscany from the ninth century BC, had a highly advanced civilization; they were more involved with their families, foods, arts, and spirituality than with weaponry and warfare. They were easily conquered by the warring empire-builders from Rome in 510 BC. The Romans were impressed by the achievements of the Etruscans. In fact, many advances that history has credited to the Romans were actually Etruscan—the technology for constructing roads, bridges, and aqueducts, for example, as well as many developments in art and science.

But the achievements of the Romans cannot be underestimated. Tracing many modern American values, concepts, and institutions back in time, we find that they have their roots in the twelve hundred years of the great Roman Empire—from the seventh century BC to the fifth century AD. Roman legacies such as laws and urban planning are still very much with us today. As the empire spread, so did its ideas regarding citizens, liberty, equality, justice, and government by law. These concepts became the basis for British law and the United States Bill of Rights, and they permeate many dimensions of our modern lives.

But even the great Roman Empire could not last forever. Gradually Rome lost control of its farflung conquests and began a long, downward spiral. By the fourth century, Germanic invaders were rampaging through Italy, and war, famine, and plague were ravaging the population.

With the fall of Rome, Italy entered the Middle Ages, which lasted from the fifth century to the end of the eleventh century. Then, from the fragmented Italian peninsula, a new civilization was born. This renaissance, or rebirth, began in small, self-governing communities. The community elected city officials to assemblies called parliaments, from Middle English and Old French *parlement*, from *parler*, meaning "to speak." There the citizens met to discuss public matters and vote on issues.

These communities developed into city-states, which moved Italy from authoritarian rule toward political, economic, and intellectual freedom. The city-states encouraged personal expression as well, and from this flowed the great variety and excellence of art and science that characterized the Renaissance. From the mid-eleventh to the mid-sixteenth century, Italy nurtured some of the greatest artists, writers, and scientists the world has known—people like Leonardo da Vinci, Michelangelo, Botticelli, Raphael, Titian, Dante, and Galileo.

The Renaissance did not stop in Italy. It sparked creative minds across the rest of Europe and, indirectly, initiated the French Revolution, the American Revolution, and other future democratic movements.

Early Arrivals in the Americas

After the Renaissance, Italy was still divided. French Bourbons ruled in the south, German Hapsburgs in the north, and the Roman Catholic papacy in central Italy. The first Italians who came to the Americas were sponsored by other European governments. These first arrivals were adventurers, explorers, warriors, sailors, and missionaries. The Italian influence began with Cristoforo Colombo, who was soon followed by Giovanni Caboto, Amerigo Vespucci, and Giovanni da Verrazano. All of them were "Italian," even though "Italy" was not yet a nation. Giovanni da Verrazano, sailing under a French flag in 1524, became the first European to see Staten Island, now a part of New York City.

Most of the Italians who came to the west and southwest of North America were missionaries. They came to spread their Roman Catholic religion among the native people. Brother Marcos de Niza arrived in 1531 and was stationed in Mexico. From there he explored the territories that would become Arizona and New Mexico. Father Eusebio Francisco Kino also combined missionary work with exploration, mapping Spain's North American empire from the Colorado River to the Gulf of Mexico. From 1698 to 1711 he founded twenty-four ranches and missions, introducing livestock, grain, fruits, and vegetables. In 1679 Henry de Tonti joined René-Robert Cavelier, sieur de La Salle, in a French expedition to Quebec, the Great Lakes, and down the Mississippi River. Over two centuries after de Tonti's journeys, Italian immigrants to Arkansas named their community Tontitown, in honor of their countryman, the first European to set foot in the state.

In the American colonies on the East Coast, most of the early Italian arrivals were weavers, gardeners, cabinetmakers, musicians, artisans, and businessmen. The colonists knew they needed people with certain knowledge and expertise, so they encouraged the emigration of Italians from the affluent, educated classes of the great cities of the Renaissance: Florence, Naples, Venice, and Rome. In 1610, for example, the colony of Virginia invited Italian winegrowers to help start their vineyards, and in 1622 the colonists sent for Venetians to help them with their glassworks and silk industry.

A number of Italians participated in the American Revolution. Francesco Vigo, who fought from 1774 to 1779, was the first Italian to become an American citizen. Most Italians who took part in the revolution were enlisted men. Two regiments of volunteers were recruited in Italy. But it was an intellectual and a writer, Filippo Mazzei, a friend of Thomas Jefferson and James Madison, who became the Italian most identified with the American Revolution.

Mazzei met Benjamin Franklin and John Adams in England, and they persuaded him to visit the colony of Virginia. There, Mazzei's longtime sympathy for the colonies blossomed into enthusiasm. With Jefferson, his friend and translator, he published essays under the pen name Furioso in the *Virginia Gazette*. One of those articles, translated by Jefferson, included words that were to be echoed in the Declaration of Independence: "*Tutti gli uomini sono per natura egulmente liberi e independenti*—All men are by nature equally free and independent." Mazzei went on to write: "Such equality is necessary in order to create a free government. A true Republican government cannot exist unless all men from the richest to the poorest are perfectly equal in their natural rights."[2]

---

[2] Di Franco, Philip. *The Italian American Experience* (New York: Tor Books, 1988).

Mazzei wanted to join the Continental Army, but Jefferson persuaded him to go back to Europe instead and raise money and support for the revolution. Mazzei did so, living in Paris and writing many pamphlets for the American cause. When the colonists declared their autonomy from Britain, Jefferson sent Mazzei a handwritten copy of the Declaration of Independence in recognition of his influence on the political philosophy of the new nation.

The First Wave of Immigrants

The adventurers and explorers from Italy gave way in the mid-eighteenth century to permanent settlers. Approximately twelve thousand Italians came to the United States between its founding in 1776 and the establishment of the modern Italian nation in 1870. These were mostly artists, sculptors, stoneworkers, musicians, teachers, and political refugees.

Lorenzo da Ponte introduced opera to the United States. A composer in Italy, he came to the United States in 1804 and was the first professor of Italian Language and Literature at Columbia University in New York. In 1833, he raised money to build the nation's first opera house. He then invited Italian opera companies to perform the first two operas many Americans had ever heard: *The Barber of Seville* and *Don Giovanni.*

Although Alexander Graham Bell is commonly credited with inventing the telephone, it was an Italian immigrant, Antonio Meucci, who built the first telephone in 1849. Meucci was too poor to take out a patent, so Bell's invention is the one we recognize today. Meucci tried to sue Bell but lost in court in 1887.

Few people know that it was the vision and craftsmanship of an immigrant, Constantino Brumidi, that gave the United States Capitol much of its grandeur. A political refugee, Brumidi had been a well-known fresco painter in Italy. Upon his arrival in the United States in 1852, he began decorating the Capitol. For the next twenty years he worked steadily, designing bronze staircases, creating marble statues, and painting intricate frescoes such as *Cincinnatus at the*

Plough and *Apotheosis of Washington* on the walls and ceilings of the Capitol. For two years, he lay on his back 180 feet above the floor to paint a 4,664-square-foot mural on the interior of the dome.

As an old man, he wrote: "I have no longer any desire for fame or fortune. My one ambition and my daily prayer is that I may live long enough to make beautiful the Capitol of the one Country in the World in which there is liberty."[3]

The Italian Revolution

The successful American struggle for independence was a victory for the ancient Etruscan and Roman values of liberty and equality. Ironically, the land in which these values were born and first put into practice was still under foreign rule. But in the mid-1800s, four men began to lead the *Risorgimento*, the "Reorganization," or drive for a unified, independent Italy. King Victor Emmanuel II, Count Camillo Benso di Cavour, Giuseppe Mazzini, and Giuseppe Garibaldi struggled for more than twenty years to achieve a unified Italy, free of foreign rulers, whose government would be based on democratic principles.

Of the four main figures of the *Risorgimento*, Garibaldi is the most famous. He was an idealistic hero-adventurer who left school at fifteen to work as a cabin boy on a Russian ship. After taking part in an early, ill-fated drive for Italian independence, Garibaldi fled to Brazil to avoid being imprisoned. There he tried to earn a living as a trader, but failed miserably. When he heard that a southern Brazilian province was waging a war for independence, he became a member of its tiny navy, wreaking havoc on Brazilian shipping. In the skirmishes, Garibaldi freed all the Afro-Brazilian slaves he encountered.

After fourteen years of wandering in Latin America as a warrior for freedom, Garibaldi returned to Italy in 1848. His battles against the French in his homeland were futile, how-

---

[3] Murdock, Myrtle Cheney. *Constantino Brumidi* (Washington, D.C.: Monumental Press, 1950).

Many Italian emigrants left the "old country" because they felt that it offered them only backbreaking work and poverty. The faces of these new arrivals from Italy capture the mixture of anxiety and optimism many emigrants must have felt.

ever, and he fled again, this time to Staten Island in New York. From there he followed developments in Italy, including reports of terrible suffering and oppression in Sicily.

In 1860 Garibaldi returned to Italy and hastily put together a band of soldiers, dressing them in bright red shirts. Garibaldi and his Red Shirts were victorious in Sicily, and Garibaldi became an instant hero. Pictures of him as the liberator of southern Italy hung in many American homes. After liberating Sicily, Garibaldi charged victoriously into Naples and then marched on to take Rome.

Here, however, he was stopped by forces of his ally, Victor Emmanuel, who feared the French would intervene to save the pope and did not want to risk the lives of the Red Shirts. In 1867 Garibaldi tried again to take Rome, but French forces rebuffed him. By 1870, however, the French forces were weak from their defeats in the Franco-Prussian war. Finally, on September 20, 1870, Garibaldi and his Red

Shirts marched victoriously into Rome, and on July 2, 1871, Rome was proclaimed capital of a united Italy.

Unification and Division

Peace and prosperity did not come quickly or easily to the new nation. Neither did a sense of national loyalty. An Italian statesman commented: "Now that they have made Italy, they will have to make Italians."

The main factor interfering with true unification was the long and deep division between "the two Italys"—the north and the south. The northerners considered themselves superior because of their higher education and greater wealth, which resulted from their region's industrialization. At the beginning of the twentieth century, 75 percent of southern Italians were illiterate. The popular conception in the north was that southerners were stupid, shiftless, and lazy. But the people of the south, which was known as the *Mezzogiorno*, were simply much poorer and less well educated than those in the north because of many factors beyond their control. While the northerners attended school and concerts, the southerners slaved in their landlords' fields. While the northerners ate meat and vegetables, the southerners ate little more than pasta and bread.

The mass of Sicilians, Calabrians, and other southern Italians who had accepted Garibaldi as their liberator assumed that soon their economic and social situation would improve. But their hopes were dashed as the new government ignored their problems and even introduced new taxes. In the turbulent early decades of the Italian nation, the southerners' feelings about their new government were summed up in two words: *ladro governo*—a thief of a government.

One of the ironic facts of Italy's history is that within fifty years of the nation's unification, 5 million Italians emigrated to the United States.

La Miseria of the *Mezzogiorno*

The history of most Italian Americans begins with an ances-

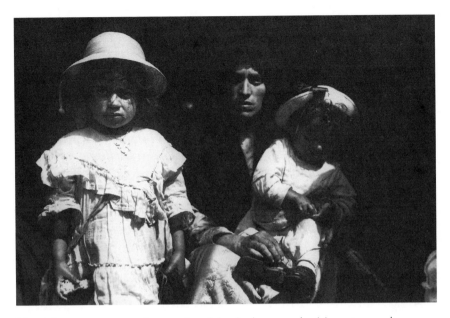

Most Italian immigrants came from southern Italy, also known as the *Mezzogiorno*, where economic conditions and limited education presented formidable barriers to progress for many peasants. This Italian woman and her daughters arrived in Boston in 1921.

tor's decision to emigrate. Most emigrants were from the poor regions of the *Mezzogiorno*, where many had lived in one-room dwellings with earthen floors and no windows. They had been working in their landlords' fields twelve to sixteen hours a day and surviving on a meager diet of potatoes, corn, and dried pepper. Rocco Morelli, an immigrant who arrived in the United States in 1920, remembered his mother telling him why they were leaving Italy, "I do not want to raise my children in this country any longer. I don't want wars. I don't want no poverty. I want to go to the United States. You work over there. The children will work over there. And at least we'll eat."[4] Variations on this theme of poverty and suffering at home and the promise of riches abroad—or at least a job—were echoed by many other immigrants.

[4] Chermayeff, Ivan, et al. *Ellis Island: An Illustrated History of the Immigrant Experience* (New York: Macmillan, 1991).

After unification, misgovernment, as well as a rapid growth in population, made it harder than ever to find food and jobs. Making matters worse, diseases such as cholera and malaria ravaged the population. Malaria was a side effect of extensive deforestation, soil erosion, and drainage problems, conditions that led to swamps—ideal places for malarial mosquitoes to breed. In addition to overpopulation and plagues, the Italians suffered through natural disasters such as droughts, earthquakes, and volcanic eruptions. The last straw for some was a fungal disease that devastated the grape harvests many families depended on for their livelihood.

Although the unification of Italy was supposed to have improved the lives of all Italians, in fact it improved only the lives of the northerners. This intensified the conflict between north and south. Many men and women from the south, worn out and discouraged, still had no land and could not make a living. When the new central government imposed even higher taxes, the best alternative seemed simply to leave.

Within a few years of unification, Italians were packing their few belongings and leaving their ancestral lands for the United States. More than 4 million Italians migrated from 1870 to 1920, more than 80 percent of them from the *Mezzogiorno*. A European traveler in southern Italy in the nineteenth century reported that the only decorations he had seen in the homes of Sicilian peasants were "advertisements of steamship lines to the United States and South America."

Rocco Boffilo, a Calabrian peasant or *contadino*, described his situation: "Things go badly here. Many *contadini* here do not eat bread. . . . One can only find work three or four months out of the year. Why do so many go to America? Because they are better off there. The work here, in comparison, is too much to bear. Up at sunrise, carrying your tools while walking several kilometers to the fields and then returning during the darkness in the evening, totally exhausted: that is the life we live here."[5]

---

[5] La Sorte, Michael. *La Merica: Images of the Italian Greenhorn Experience* (Philadelphia: Temple University Press, 1985).

The fledgling Italian government had mixed feelings about the many citizens leaving for America. On the one hand, they knew that the impoverished peasants had good reasons to leave and that the money they earned in America would trickle back to the families and villages they left behind. As early as 1877, the Italian government helped Italian Americans send money back to Italy with money orders instead of entrusting their cash to the mail.

As the tide of immigrants became a flood, however, some members of the government began to worry. In 1878, when an Italian government minister issued a decree urging people not to leave their nation, a group of peasants sent him this reply:

> What do you mean by a nation, Mr. Minister? ... We plant and we reap wheat but never do we eat white bread. We cultivate the grape but we drink no wine. We raise animals for food but we eat no meat. We are clothed in rags. ... And in spite of all this, you counsel us, Mr. Minister, not to abandon our country. But is that land, where one cannot live by toil, one's country?[6]

As the first immigrants to the United States sent back reports of the jobs to be found and the money to be earned, more and more people decided to make the journey. Soon whole villages were leaving. In 1902, an Italian reported that the peasants of a Sicilian village gathered one day at the gate to their landlord's estate. There they threw down their shovels and posted a notice: "Sir, do your farming yourself—we are going to America."

The Main Migration

Although life in southern Italy and Sicily was nearly unbearable, it was still hard for emigrants to say goodbye to loved ones and the only life they had ever known. Before the turn of the century nearly everyone was born, married, and

---

[6] Hoobler, Dorothy, and Hoobler, Thomas. *The Italian American Family Album* (New York: Oxford University Press, 1994).

Departure to the United States could be a wrenching experience for Italian emigrants, many of whom had lived in the same villages their entire lives. These three young emigrants had grown up in the same Italian town. After arriving in the United States, they had to say good-bye to each other as their parents took them to different parts of the country.

buried in the same town. Many Italians who came to the United States had never before ventured any farther than the next village up the road. Imagine the courage it must have taken for your ancestors to leave a family, a culture, and a way of life so deeply rooted in a particular place.

Mary Nick Juliano recalled leaving San Giovanni in Fiore, Calabria: "There was a little scene in front of our home there in Italy that I'll never forget. I hung on to Grandma Sucurro, and that's just as vivid as today. I wouldn't let go. It took two or three to unwrap my little arms. I was just five. And I screamed her name. My uncle grabbed me and hugged me tight. And the last thing I remember—is—that dear, dear little grandma, falling on the cobblestone road, screaming my name."[7]

The emigrants bade farewell to the comfort and security of all they had ever known to set out for a land that was little more than a rumor. An Italian author, Edmondo DeAmicis, sailed to the United States in 1890. He described the scene as the peasants boarded the ship *Galileo* at the port of Genoa.

> Workmen, peasants, women with children at the breast, little fellows with the tin medal of the infant asylum still hanging around their necks passed on their way, and almost everyone was carrying something. They had folding chairs, they had bags and trunks of every shape in their hands or on their heads; their arms were full of mattresses and bedclothes, and their berth tickets were held fast in their mouths.[8]

At the seaports of Genoa, Naples, and Palermo many emigrants caught the last glimpse of their loved ones. Luciano de Cresenzo remembers a farewell custom: "Many immigrants had brought on board balls of yarn, leaving one

---

[7] Taylor, David A., and Williams, John Alexander, eds. *Old Ties, New Attachments: Italian-American Folklife in the West* (Washington, D.C.: Library of Congress, 1992).

[8] DeAmicis, Edmondo. *On Blue Water*. Trans. by Jacob B. Brown (New York: Putnam, 1907).

end of the line with someone on land. As the ship slowly cleared the dock, the balls unwound amid the farewell shouts of the women, the fluttering of the handkerchiefs, and the infants held high. After the yarn ran out, the long strips remained airborne, sustained by the wind, long after those on land and those at sea had lost sight of each other."[9]

Today, you can fly from the eastern part of the United States to Italy in about seven hours. In the late nineteenth and early twentieth centuries, however, the journey was made on a steamship and took about two weeks. It was not a luxury cruise, but an arduous ordeal. One emigrant noted that the sea passage "seems to have been so calculated as to inflict upon us the last, full measure of suffering and indignity. ..." The journey across the Atlantic became known as *"la via dolorosa,"* the sorrowful way.

Most emigrants traveled in steerage—the section below decks for the passengers with the cheapest tickets. There they were crammed in overcrowded berths and fed little but thin soup and hard bread. Some passengers brought bundles of food from home to sustain them. With the cramped quarters, foul air, bad food, and rough seas, the journey was difficult and often terrifying—particularly to peasants whose only previous travel had been on mule from one small town to another.

Angelo Pellegrini recalls the voyage from Genoa to New York:

> It was a rough passage ... Day after day, for three long weeks, the scene never changed: the same faces, pale with sickness and with fear, stared vacantly, or cast furtive glances at one another, as if each sought reassurance in the presence of his doomed companions. An elderly woman ... complained of her misery to a member of the crew. When he assured her that she would not die she shot back

---

[9] La Sorte, op. cit.

at him, with unintended humor, that he had taken from her her last hope.[10]

After two to three weeks on the high seas, the Italian immigrants caught the first glimpse of their new nation. For many this glimpse was the thrilling sight of the Statue of Liberty, its torch held high. More than 95 percent of Italian immigrants followed the path first sailed by the fifteenth-century explorer Giovanni da Verrazano, passing between Brooklyn and Staten Island to arrive in New York City.

In the first years of immigration, the arrivals simply filed down the gangplank of the ship and into the streets of New York. They were immediately surrounded by "runners" from boardinghouses, railways, and banks. Each runner quoted lower exchange rates for their *lira* (Italian currency) and lower prices for lodging. Only later did the immigrants learn they had "misunderstood." Because so many immigrants fell prey to these swindlers, New York State officials opened a landing station in an old amusement park called Castle Garden. Here the new arrivals could exchange their money at honest rates, buy railroad tickets to other destinations, and get information about lodging and employment.

Ellis Island

As the stream of immigrants grew, U.S. officials moved from helping immigrants enter the United States to blocking entry to those who might be "a burden" on society. In 1890 the federal government took over the processing of immigrants, and on January 1, 1892, the Ellis Island immigration station opened.

Ocean liners at the turn of the century held about six thousand passengers each. Upon arrival, the steerage passengers were herded into small ferryboats and taken to Ellis Island. The first- and second-class passengers were not detained. At Ellis Island, uniformed officials examined the

---

[10] Pellegrini, Angelo. *American Dream: An Immigrant's Quest* (San Francisco: North Point Press, 1986).

immigrants to weed out the sick or lame, those without money, and anyone else they deemed unfit. The process was confusing, humiliating, and frightening to the new immigrants. As family members were separated from one another or were overcome by fear and frustration, many broke down and cried. Thus Ellis Island became known to the Italians as *Isola della Lacrime*, the island of tears.

Although only a mile of water separated the immigrants from the United States, some would never come ashore. Keeping their precious possessions with them, they shuffled forward in long lines, moving from one examiner to the next. A cough, a limp, or slowness of speech might be enough to send them back to Italy. Giulio Mirando reported, "In the doctor's hand was a piece of chalk; on the coats of about two out of every ten or eleven immigrants who passed him he scrawled a large white letter H for possible heart trouble, L for lameness, a circled X for suspected mental defects, or F for a bad rash on the face."[11]

Those with chalk marks had to submit to further examination or quarantine. Those who passed the physical examination then had to answer dozens of rapid-fire questions: Where are you going? Do you have a job? What kind of work can you do? Is anyone waiting for you? and so on. If the person answered correctly, the inspector signed an approval form, often shortening or changing the "difficult" Italian names. About 2 percent of the new arrivals were deemed unfit in some way and were sent back to Italy.

In 1914, World War I reduced the flow of immigrants. By the time the war ended in 1918, legislators who opposed immigration had gained a majority in Congress. In 1921, a temporary federal law limited the number of immigrants allowed to enter the United States. Then, in 1924, a more comprehensive law set a limit of 150,000 European immigrants per year. From 1924 to 1945 Italian immigration slowed to between five thousand and six thousand a year.

Over the more than forty years that Ellis Island processed

---

[11] Mangione and Morreale, op. cit.

immigrants, nearly one-third of the 12 million people who passed through its doors were Italian. Census figures for 1990 show that of the nearly 15 million Americans who identified their ancestry as Italian, the great majority came through Ellis Island or were descendants of those who did.

Land of Plenty, Land of Prejudice

Angelo Pellegrini and his family arrived in New York in 1913. Although passing through customs at Ellis Island was "a nightmare," a treat awaited them. "At long last we had arrived in America! ... We debarked, of course, at Ellis Island, though we then knew nothing about it, nor about its purpose, nor about the annoying routine to which all aliens who entered America had to submit." After passing through all the examinations, the Pellegrinis went to a restaurant. "And this is what we were served: sliced oranges, ham, eggs, fried potatoes, buttered toast, coffee, cream, sugar. And would we have more toast? Just ask for it. Would we have more coffee, more cream? Just ask for them. As much as we could eat of anything. All for one price. ... We had hoped for much from the New World. But we had not hoped for all that."[12]

For many, America represented a dreamland of plentiful food and "sweet money," *dolci dollari*. But of course, dreams and reality are seldom the same. One immigrant recalled, "I came to America because I heard the streets were paved with gold. When I got here, I found out three things: first, the streets weren't paved with gold; second, they weren't paved at all; and third, I was expected to pave them."[13]

The Italian immigrants did pave roads. They also worked in factories and mines and built bridges and subways. But even while they contributed to the nation, like most other immigrants, Italians were called derogatory names and looked down upon. Fiorello LaGuardia, who became the

---

[12] Pellegrini, op. cit.
[13] Hoobler and Hoobler, op. cit.

Subway workers toil beneath New York City's Eighth Avenue in 1932. Italian Americans contributed much of the labor that went into subway construction.

mayor of New York City, recalls in his autobiography: "I must have been about ten when a street organ-grinder with a monkey blew into town. He, and particularly the monkey, attracted a great deal of attention. I can still hear the cries of the kids: 'A dago with a monkey! Hey Fiorello, you're a dago too. Where's your monkey?' It hurt. . . . I couldn't understand it. What difference was there between us? Some of their families hadn't been in the country any longer than mine."[14]

Even Italians who never learned English knew that the terms *wop* and *dago* were derogatory. No one is sure of the origin of these words. In Neapolitan dialect, *guappo* (woppo) means a young man who thinks a bit too highly of himself and dresses to show it. When such a person strutted the streets of New York City in a fancy new suit he could hear

---

[14] LaGuardia, Fiorello H. *Fiorello H. LaGuardia, The Making of an Insurgent* (New York: Capricorn Books, 1961).

"*guappo*" from Italians. Everybody else heard it too, and soon "wop" became the epithet for all Italians. Other scholars say that the word *wop* came from the phrase "without passport." *Dago* might have been a pidgin English term for a day's labor (day-go).

Name-calling was far from the worst form of prejudicial treatment that the Italian immigrants suffered. In 1891, nine Sicilians in New Orleans were acquitted by a jury on charges of killing the chief of police and were sent back to prison to await further charges. A mob stormed the jail. Eleven Italians—the nine who were acquitted and two others—were dragged outside and lynched. Organizations such as the American Protective Association, founded in Clinton, Iowa, in 1887, were often responsible for whipping up anti-Catholic and anti-Italian sentiment, as they sought to "safeguard" the Protestant, Anglo-Saxon character of the United States against "Romanism." Italians were also convenient scapegoats for ills ranging from impoverished slums to government corruption and class conflict.

Birds of Passage

Despite the discrimination and prejudice they faced, the Italians continued to come to the United States. Unlike early immigrants who were mostly skilled artisans, those who immigrated after 1870 were generally unskilled laborers. Most of them were men who came to find jobs, save up some money, and return to the old country.

During the decades of the mass migration, the United States was thriving and expanding. The expansion demanded more roads, railroads, sewage and water pipelines, and buildings. The Italians were a willing workforce, laying railroad track, building streets and subways, hacking stone from quarries, and working long hours in factories.

Between 1900 and 1910, more than 2 million Italians entered the United States. About half returned to Italy. Though some Italian workers went to farms in the South and West, most remained on the East Coast and took work they described as "pick-a-shovel." From 1880 to 1930 Ital-

Italian Americans went to work on farms, in factories, in mines, and a variety of other fields. Some were entrepreneurs, like this grocery store owner on New York's Mulberry Street, a predominantly Italian neighborhood.

ian Americans dug, cut, harvested, mined, and worked in factories and steel mills. They were also organ grinders and pushcart vendors. Workers returning to Italy complained about the cold climate and the harsh bosses in America, but not about the dollars they had saved. Most men could live on half their earnings and save the other half to buy small plots of land or shops back in Italy.

In New York, Italians helped construct the modern city's skyscrapers, bridges, tunnels, subways, and streets. In a moment of candor, a city official said in 1890, "We can't get along without Italians. We want someone to do the dirty work."[15] Italians were paid much less than others doing the same work. In 1910 the average Italian-born male made $396 a year compared with the national average of $666 a year.

Even though Italians willingly did the "dirty work" for low wages, some Americans complained about the presence of "foreign labor." When President Woodrow Wilson was told that Italians should be kept out of the United States because they always returned home and took their dollars with them, Wilson replied: "They took their dollars, but they left the subways."[16]

The Italian workers also left many bridges, roads, and buildings. The "birds of passage" worked hard and took great pride in physical labor. A third-generation Italian American said, "The only time I really felt close to my grandfather was when he drove me past a post office in Brooklyn. He had to stop the car and get out and explain how he helped build it—put the cornerstone in. The way he talked about it—he was so happy, so thrilled to be part of it. It was like it meant more to him than anything else he had ever done."[17]

Many men who came to the United States intending to

[15] Hoobler and Hoobler, op. cit.

[16] Nelli, Humbert. *From Immigrants to Ethnics: The Italian Americans* (Oxford: Oxford University Press, 1983).

[17] Mangione and Morreale, op. cit.

return to Italy ended up staying. One pair of brothers was representative: "We had said that when we saved $1,000 each we would go back to Italy and buy a farm, but now that the time is coming we are so busy and making so much money that we think we will stay."

The *Padrone* System

When the Italians passed through Ellis Island and stepped onto the mainland, they also often stepped into the hands of the *padrone*, or boss. The *padrone* had come over earlier and learned the language and the labor needs of the new country. He was paid to hire workers for specific projects and send them to the work site.

But the *padroni* were generally more than simply job brokers. Within the immigrant community, the *padroni* served as interpreters, bankers, real estate agents, and advisors. They assisted people in sending money to families in Italy. A *padrone* could help find housing, act as a notary, lend money, and cope with courts and legal matters.

Some *padroni* also exploited newcomers. An employer would pay the workers' wages to the *padrone*, who would then pay a fraction of the amount to the workers. Sensational reports in the American press described *padroni* who purchased or stole poor Italian children and brought them to the United States as slaves to work the streets as musicians, bootblacks, acrobats, and beggars.

One of the most famous *padroni* was Jim Marsh (born Antonio Michelino Maggio). He came to New York in 1873 and soon mastered English. He seized the opportunity to become a *padrone* during a railroad strike in 1880. Because he could speak English to management and Italian to the workers, Marsh was able to settle the dispute. Soon he was bringing more new Italian immigrants to the railroad and to other employers.

The *padroni* of the time were called many things: boss, king, shylock, thief. Still, they met a critical demand, bringing workers ignorant of all aspects of the American labor market to employers eager to hire them. Some *padroni* even went back to Italy to persuade people to emigrate. They found workers, paid for their passage, and then found them jobs. Often they exploited them by using them as strike-breakers.

To stop such exploitation, Italy created the Commissariat of Emigration in 1901. This agency assisted and protected Italian immigrants—particularly from the "buzzard-like *padrone*" who would seek to entrap then in "peonage." Many "mutual aid societies" were also founded. By 1912, Chicago alone had four hundred mutual aid societies. These societies were staffed by established immigrants and provided assistance to recent immigrants.

While men far outnumbered women immigrants in the earlier years, later more and more women came. They often went to work in clothing factories. Joseph Costanzo described his mother's work in a mill: "My mother was a twister in the Lawrence mills. It was unusual; in Italy there were no jobs for women. In fact, people that heard about it back in the village didn't like the idea of the women working. But my mother felt she was doing no different from all the women, so she decided she was going to work. Make some money."[18]

The immigrant women also suffered exploitation. Agnes Santucci recalled: "The machine used to go, keep agoing, keep agoing. I was so unhappy to stay there all day, not go out like it was a prison. I couldn't speak English. I used to stay at the machine all day without seeing anybody. The forelady used to be back and forth, back and forth, look this way, look the other way. Do your work, do your work. An Italian girl fell asleep at the machine and she was fired."[19]

Labor Leaders and Anarchists

But Italian Americans, heirs to a great cultural and intellectual tradition, resisted exploitation. They were very active in

---

[18] Chermayeff et al., op. cit.

[19] Ewen, Elizabeth. *Immigrant Women in the Land of Dollars* (New York: Monthly Review Press, 1985).

Nicola Sacco and Bartolomeo Vanzetti, Italian American workers and anarchists, were wrongly convicted of murder in 1920. They were executed seven years later, victims of a judge's anti-foreigner bias.

labor unions that fought for better wages and working conditions, such as the Industrial Workers of the World, the United Textile Workers of America, and the Clothing Workers of America. Luigi Antonini helped found the International Ladies' Garment Workers' Union, and Frank Bellanca was instrumental in starting the Amalgamated Clothing and Textile Workers of America. Italian Americans led strikes by mineworkers in the Western states, by silkworkers in New Jersey, and by textile workers in New England. Carlo Tresca was a labor agitator who participated in many strikes. He also founded *Il Martello*, a journal that exposed management abuses. A small number of Italian American laborers were anarchists, opposing any kind of organized government.

One of the most famous and heartbreaking cases of injustice against Italian Americans was that of Nicola Sacco and Bartolomeo Vanzetti. On April 15, 1920, two men were killed in a payroll robbery in South Braintree, Massachusetts. Soon two naturalized American citizens, Sacco and Vanzetti, were arrested and charged with the crime, even though no incriminating material evidence was found. Sacco was a factory worker and was at the Italian consulate in Boston when the crime occurred; Vanzetti was a fish peddler, who was selling fish at the time of the murders. But Sacco and Vanzetti were anarchists, like many other laborers of the time. Along with their immigrant status, this fact made them vulnerable to the antiforeign hysteria that followed World War I.

After a trial conducted by Judge Webster Thayer, a man who had often bluntly proclaimed his hatred for foreigners and "Reds," Sacco and Vanzetti were found guilty and sentenced to death. At his sentencing Vanzetti declared:

> Not only am I innocent of these two crimes, not only in all my life I have never stole, never killed, never spilled blood, but I have struggled all my life, since I began to reason, to eliminate crime from the earth. . . .
>
> We have proved that there could not have been another judge on the face of the earth more prejudiced and more cruel than you have been against us. We have proven that. Still they refuse the new trial. We know, and you know in your heart, that you have been against us from the very beginning, before you see us. . . . I have suffered because I was an Italian, and indeed I am an Italian; I have suffered more for my family and for my beloved than for myself; but I am so convinced to be right that if you could execute me two times, and if I could be reborn two other times, I would live again to do what I have done already.
>
> I have finished. Thank you.[20]

On August 27, 1927, the two were put to death, still maintaining their innocence. Fifty years later, Massachusetts Governor Michael Dukakis declared August 23, 1978, a memorial day for Sacco and Vanzetti.

---

[20] Mangione and Morreale, op. cit.

The Sacco-Vanzetti case became a crossroads for some Italian immigrants and their children. If this was how their adoptive country was going to treat them, they thought, it was not worth even trying to live an honest life. It may not have been a coincidence that around this time some young, ambitious Italian Americans turned their energies to crime rather than to politics or honest work as a way out of the ghetto.

Prohibition and Gangsters

Italians immigrated in large numbers between 1880 and 1920—the years when the American temperance movement was at a peak. Perhaps no other element of their adopted country's mentality puzzled Italians more. From childhood they had consumed wine as an enjoyable part of every meal except breakfast. Moderate drinking was not a vice in Italy. The American movement to ban all alcohol, with the misleading name "temperance movement," made little sense to most Italian newcomers.

The Eighteenth Amendment to the U.S. Constitution, prohibiting the sale of all alcohol, became effective in 1920. A Sicilian proverb states that where the law is made, fraud comes forth (*Fatta la legge nasce l'inganno*). This was certainly true after Prohibition. Some Italians, as well as many Americans of other ethnicities, quickly recognized the potential profits in liquor and became involved in the illegal manufacture, sale, and distribution of alcoholic beverages.

The involvement sometimes led to conflicts within families. The father of a working-class family in the Italian community on the South Side of Chicago agreed to let bootleggers store their liquor in his garage. "This enraged Ma," her daughter remembers, "who did not want her home harboring illegal alcohol. But once the gangsters began using the garage, Pa had no choice but to continue the arrangement. After many arguments Ma hit on the idea of tearing down the garage—no garage, no liquor, no problems—and that's what she did."

Other illegal ventures operated along the fringes of boot-

Italian-born Frank Costello resented the drudgery and discrimination that characterized his parents' lives. He sought to improve his fortunes with the "easy money" to be had in gambling and selling liquor. Above, Costello leaves an investigating committee's offices in 1954.

legging—gambling, prostitution, and racketeering. The same personnel and communication systems began to serve them all. Most Italians stayed outside the criminal network, continuing to earn their pay with long, backbreaking days of work. But in the public's mind, a few examples such as Al Capone and Frank Costello tagged an entire people. To many, an Italian surname hinted an association with the Mafia long after Prohibition ended.

Frank Costello, one of the most notorious of the gangsters, came to the United States when he was nine and grew up in a New York City slum. At sixteen he ran away from home and his hardworking but poor parents. Like some American sons of Italian peasants, Costello despised his father's humility and hard work. He wanted to escape his father's grocery stand and grab the easy money in gambling and bootlegging. By 1923, Costello helped to command a vast operation that illegally shipped liquor from Canada in a dozen speedboats armed with machine guns and aided by corrupt members of the Coast Guard. The story goes that once Costello's swift vessels accidentally strayed into the path of a speedboat race, swished across the finish line first, and kept going.

Finally in 1954, Costello was convicted of tax fraud. The journalist Walter Winchell asked him, "What was the first mistake?"

"If you call it a mistake," Costello said, "I guess it was being born of poor parents and raised in a tough neighborhood. If things had been different I might have gone to college and been sitting up there with Mr. Kefauver [the U.S. senator]."[21]

Success Stories

The vast majority of Italian Americans born of poor parents and growing up in tough neighborhoods were honest and

---

[21] DiStasi, Lawrence, ed. *Dream Streets* (New York: Harper and Row, 1989).

Mother Cabrini, the first U.S. citizen to be named a saint by the Roman Catholic Church, came to the United States as a young nun in 1889 and devoted herself to helping the poor of New York's Little Italy.

hard-working. Although Costello, Capone, and Lucky Luciano received more press, the average Italian American steered clear of criminal activities. Most worked diligently in garment factories, wholesale food companies, grocery stores, restaurants, steel mills, and the construction industry. Some of these men and women became American success stories.

Sister Frances Xavier Cabrini arrived in New York's Lower East Side in 1889. She spent her first night in the United States in a mouse-infested room. Expecting to find a convent ready to house her small order of five sisters, she called on New York's Archbishop Michael Corrigan. At the time there was great ill-will between Irish Catholics and Italian Catholics, and the archbishop did not mince words. "My advice to you and your sisters," he said, "is to take the next boat back to Italy."[22]

Instead, Sister Cabrini stayed in New York's Little Italy. There she saw people desperately in need. First she opened an embroidery school in a basement. Then she established a nursery to keep four hundred slum children off the street. When she had saved $250, she opened a hospital for the poor, calling it Columbus Hospital. She persuaded doctors to work there part time without charging fees. Today there are seven Columbus Hospitals serving the poor in cities throughout the United States.

Mother Cabrini died in 1917 and was beatified in 1938. She was canonized in 1946, becoming the first U.S. citizen to be declared a saint by the Roman Catholic Church.

When people asked A. P. Giannini how he had transformed his little Bank of Italy into the giant Bank of America Corporation, he answered, "Well, we were new to the game when we started out; we did unusual things." The "unusual things" included following farmers around in their fields and persuading them to take their money from under their mattresses or behind the loose brick in the chimney and put it in the bank.

---

[22] Ibid.

"They used to say I was undignified," he said of his competitors. "Old fogies! I say, if you want something, you may as well go after it."[23]

After the great San Francisco earthquake of 1906, all the banks closed or refused to lend money. Giannini seized the opportunity to put his desk out on a ruined pier. There he began accepting deposits and making loans. By taking banking to the people and by pioneering the system of branch banking, Giannini became one of the most successful Italian Americans on the West Coast. The Bank of America has over five hundred branches in the United States today.

Three Italian émigrés have won the Nobel Prize—two nuclear physicists and a molecular biologist. All three came to the United States because of the anti-Jewish policies of Benito Mussolini.

Enrico Fermi, the man who was to launch the atomic age, was born in Rome in 1901. He became fascinated by physics at an early age, and by the time he entered the University of Pisa in 1918 he was more knowledgeable than most of his professors. He published many important findings in the 1920s and 1930s. When Mussolini passed a series of anti-Jewish regulations in 1938, Fermi feared for the safety of his Jewish wife, Laura. At about the same time, Fermi learned that he was to be awarded the 1938 Nobel Prize in Physics. He and his wife decided to go to Stockholm and accept the prize and then sail for New York instead of returning to Italy.

In the United States, Fermi began working on the first step in creating an atomic bomb, a self-sustaining chain reaction. Fermi designed the experiment, and forty-two of the world's leading atomic physicists were on hand as he gave the orders. When it became apparent that the experiment was successful, the physicist Arthur Compton delivered the message to a Harvard University professor through a

---

[23] DiStasi, op. cit.

prearranged code that referred to another Italian, Christopher Columbus:

"The Italian navigator has landed in the New World." "How were the natives?" asked the scientist at Harvard. "Very friendly," Compton reported.[24]

Emilio Segrè was born and raised in Tivoli, Italy. He studied with Fermi in Rome and was visiting the United States in 1938 when he learned that he and all other Jewish professors had been fired from the universities in Italy. Segrè and his family never returned to Italy. In 1959, he was awarded the Nobel Prize for his discovery of the antiproton.

Salvador Luria was born in Turin, Italy, and studied for a year with Fermi in Rome. His talents, however, were not in physics but in molecular biology. As a Jew, he was forced to flee Fascist Italy in 1938. In the United States he continued his research on spontaneous mutations. His discoveries helped lay the foundations of today's genetic engineering techniques and also improved the use of chemotherapy as a treatment for cancer. He won the Nobel Prize in 1969.

When Mussolini joined in the Nazi invasion of France, his support among Italian Americans declined. After the United States entered World War II in 1941, Americans of Italian descent swiftly showed their loyalty by volunteering for the armed forces. One of the great heroes of the war was Marine Sergeant John Basilone, whose squad fought valiantly on the island of Guadalcanal in the Pacific. For three days and nights in October 1942, he and his unit held off a whole regiment of Japanese soldiers with one machine gun. Basilone was awarded the Congressional Medal of Honor and returned home to Raritan, New Jersey. There he could think only of his companions back in the Pacific, and he asked to be returned to combat. He died in the assault on Iwo Jima in 1945.

---

[24] DiStasi, op. cit.

Italian Americans were undivided in their loyalty to the United States in World War II. Above, Italian Americans unfurl an American flag on the fire escape of a Mulberry Street apartment building following the surrender of Italy to the Allied powers in 1943. They also flew the Italian flag for the first time since the United States had entered the war against Italy and other Axis powers.

Like John Basilone, few Italian Americans hesitated in making the choice between the new country and the old. The Italian immigrants and their children had become part of the United States.

Becoming American: Something Lost, Something Gained

An Italian proverb points to what would be the main difficulty for first-generation Italian Americans: "He who gives up the old ways for the new ones knows what he has lost but not what lies ahead (*Chi lascia la via vecchia per la nuova sa quel che perde e non sa quel che trova*)."

In Italy, great trust and loyalty existed within the family and within small villages. This attitude was called *campanilismo*—distrust of all social, cultural, and political contacts beyond earshot of the local church's belltower, or *campanile.* Even after they had moved thousands of miles away from Italy and their own towns' church towers, many Italians could not give up their strong feelings of *campanilismo.* These feelings helped shape settlement patterns and determine occupations in the United States.

Life in the United States was primarily an urban experience. Little Italys sprang up in major cities. The largest was on Mulberry Street in New York City. By 1900, South Philadelphia contained the second-largest Italian American community. Other sizable neighborhoods were in Boston's North End, the new West Side of Chicago, the port area of Baltimore, and San Francisco's North Beach. Here newcomers often found relatives and others who would help them get a start in America. They heard their own language spoken, found their own foods, and felt at home.

The Roman Catholic Church was another source of comfort and strength for many Italian immigrants. As soon as they settled in communities, they erected shrines to the Virgin Mary or to the patron saint of their village in Italy. They held elaborate festivities and processions on the saint's feast day. The journalist Jacob Riis described the Feast of San Donato in New York in 1899:

All the sheets of the tenement had been stretched so as to cover the ugly sheds and outhouses. Against the dark rear tenement the shrine of the saint had been erected, shutting it altogether out of sight with a wealth of scarlet and gold. Great candles and little ones, painted and beribboned, burned in a luminous grove before the altar. The sun shone down upon a mass of holiday-clad men and women, to whom it was all as a memory of home, of the beloved home across the seas.[25]

Such practices, and many other aspects of Italian Catholi-

---

[25] Moquin, Wayne, with Charles Van Doren, eds., and Francis A. J. Ianni, consulting ed. *A Documentary History of the Italian Americans* (New York: Praeger, 1974).

cism, did not sit well with the Irish Catholics, who dominated the Catholic Church in the United States at the time and who had a different view of worship. The Irish Americans were appalled by Italian Americans approaching, kissing, and caressing statues of saints, asking for favors. Conflict with the Irish-dominated church caused many Italian immigrants to build their own churches and avoid the parochial schools, sending their children to public schools instead. This turned out to be another source of heartache to first-generation Italian Americans, as their children were quickly Americanized.

Still, the older generation felt that the tightly knit Italian American communities might preserve and guard the customs and traditions of the old country from the corrupting influence of American society. The historian Rudolph Vecoli wrote, "What [the immigrants] learned of this strange country often repelled them. From their perspective, the 'Mericani appeared a foolish people, without a sense of humor, respect, or proper behavior. . . . Efforts on the part of teachers and social workers to Americanize them and their children were resented as intrusions on the sovereignty of the family."[26]

The Second Generation

A southern Italian proverb cautions, "Don't make your children better than yourself." In peasant Italy, not to "keep one's place" in a static society was a major impertinence. But the second-generation children born in the United States and educated in the public schools rejected this idea of destiny. They also resented and rejected the ways of the old country they had never known, particularly the power of the father to decide their future.

In school, second-generation children were often looked down upon because they were Italian. Even as teachers lectured on Dante, Michelangelo, and Leonardo daVinci, they did not make a connection between the land of these

[26] Mangione and Morreale, op. cit.

accomplished artists and the ancestral land of Italian American children. Many Italian American children internalized the prejudice they experienced in school and rejected their parents and their Italian heritage. Leonard Covello, an immigrant son who became an educator, wrote, "We were becoming American by learning to be ashamed of our parents."[27]

Growing up Italian at home and American outside of the home often led to an unclear sense of identity and goals. One son of immigrant parents decided to get a college education even though "in those days it was considered something of a sacrilege for an unmarried son to be leaving his family for any reason." The poet John Ciardi remembered some of the problems of growing up in his Italian-speaking family. "Italian boys, especially, became nastily indignant. That led to shouting matches in which the kids and the father, sometimes the mother, said terrible things to one another. Two or three of the boys I grew up with ran away and were never heard from again."[28]

Women's World: *La Famiglia*

Although sons of immigrants thought they had a tough time, they were generally given more freedom than daughters, and their transition to American life was easier. When a family saved to send a child to college, the sons had priority. The daughter's destiny was to marry and raise a family. Michelena Profeta, who immigrated in 1905 to enter into a marriage arranged by her father, says, "I wanted my daughters to marry and be happy, that's all."[29] That, however, was not enough for her son, Joe, whom she wanted to be a lawyer.

A mother's different wishes for her son and for her daugh-

---

[27] Covello, Leonard, with Guido D'Agostino. *The Heart Is the Teacher* (New York: McGraw-Hill, 1958).

[28] Mangione and Morreale, op. cit.

[29] Krause, Corinne Azen. *Grandmothers, Mothers, and Daughters* (Boston: Twayne, 1991).

The woman's work in the traditional Italian household included rearing children, cooking, and cleaning. First-generation Italian American women continued this tradition, though many used their domestic skills to do piecework at home. Above, an Italian American woman shops for food at a street market in 1897.

ter could be traced back to the very separate roles assigned men and women in Italy. Historically, Italian women took on subordinate roles, waiting on their husbands and sons and spending their days ironing shirts, shining shoes, cleaning, mending, and cooking. But within the home the mother reigned supreme. She managed the financial affairs, governed the conduct of the children, and provided the warmth and security that gave the family its strength. The long hours she spent preparing the sumptuous meals that are an Italian tradition were a sign of her devotion. In return, she often demanded obedience from her children.

When Italian women immigrated to the United States, they faced many changes and challenges—in family life, in work life, and in their physical environment. Compared with the small villages, warm climates, fresh air, and green fields of Italy, the urban environment of the cities of the Northeast and Midwest, with their cold winters and crowded, dark, airless tenements, was almost unbearably harsh. Even when the women got used to the different climate and living conditions, they found it difficult to become accustomed to ways men and women behaved in the United States. The first-generation Italian women did not think much of American women, who seemed to them vain, superficial, and weak, preferring to have a good time rather than to be good wives and mothers. Italian women felt that American women were not respected. They sought to keep their own daughters from becoming Americanized. But as the daughters attended American schools and made American friends, the first-generation mothers often watched powerlessly as their daughters moved away from the ways of the "old country."

As in the old country, first-generation Italian American women put the welfare of their families first. They shopped and bargained fiercely, baked bread, prepared food, washed clothes, took care of children and elderly relatives, and cleaned the house. But they also found the freedom to play a larger role in and out of the family. Many Italian-born women began working outside the home for the first time in their lives. They used skills they had learned in Italy. There, most young girls were taught dressmaking, crocheting, and weaving as part of their training for married life. When they came to the United States, Italian women found they could use these skills in jobs for the garment industry.

Before World War I, most of the work Italian American immigrant women did was piecework that they could accomplish at home. Finishing garments for nearby clothing factories was their main occupation, but they also made artificial flowers, pins, and cheap jewelry. All of this was piecework—workers were paid for the number of pieces finished. The jobs were tedious and paid little, but because the women generally had small children and could not leave their homes, they were exploited. A mother and daughter working together could make about fifty cents a day. Putting safety pins on cards paid eight to ten cents per 100 cards. Often women enlisted the help of their children or other adults who lived at home.

The son of a Sicilian immigrant recalls the work he helped his mother do:

> What you had to do was to glue tiny artificial diamonds in the holes of lapel pins. After supper my mother would clear the table, take the glass protectors off the wheels of the furniture, and pour some glue in each glass coaster. . . . Then my father brought the lapel pins and spilled them on the table. They made a huge pile . . . we'd work until after midnight.[30]

The exploitation of immigrants, especially women, led to a growing labor movement. The story of Angela and Maria Bambace is an example of the important role Italian American women played in that movement. The two sisters immigrated from southern Italy with their family and eventually settled in East Harlem, New York. There, as teenagers, Maria and Angela worked in garment district jobs. The sisters attended union meetings and listened as organizers explained how cooperative efforts could improve their lives. In 1919, the young women helped organize a citywide needleworkers' strike for better wages and working conditions. They would visit the homes of nonstrikers and talk to their families about the importance of unity. Their ability to speak with workers in their own language won many people's confidence, and later that year they helped establish an Italian local for their union.

Women in the Roman Catholic Church began to assert themselves, too. When the Apostolic Delegate to the United States withdrew the right of women to play a role in the communion ceremony, an angry Italian American nun remarked that "a woman could carry the body of Jesus in her womb for nine months, but is not deemed worthy to hold the Eucharist in her hands for even a few minutes during mass."[31]

---

[30] Mangione and Morreale, op. cit.
[31] Ibid.

Many Italian American women got an education and found jobs with or without their parents' approval. Some married early to escape the dominance of their families and to gain control of their lives. Yet many of these rushed marriages resulted in alienation and unhappiness. While men could pursue a variety of activities, women traditionally were limited to housework and menial labor.

In 1950, 77 percent of Italian American women still worked as operators in the needle trades. By 1970 this figure dropped to 25 percent. In the clerical field over the same period, this figure jumped from 8 percent to almost 40 percent. The percentage of women entering the professions moved in the same two decades from the very low figure of 2 percent to the still low figure of 9 percent. And of these 9 percent, most entered the low-paid fields of nursing, social work, and teaching.

By the third generation, however, many Italian American women began to excel in a variety of fields. Although their lives and achievements have never been as well publicized as those of Italian American men, women began following their talents to become writers, singers, actresses, politicians, and academicians.

Modern Italian American women can look for inspiration in the work of Italian writers such as Maria Messina, who portrayed the life of peasant women, and Grazia Deledda, who began publishing in 1885 when she was twenty years old and went on to write thirty books. She won the Nobel Prize for Literature in 1926.

One accomplished but unsung third-generation novelist is Tina DeRosa. In her first novel, *Paper Fish*, she tells the story of a young girl growing up in one of Chicago's largest Italian neighborhoods. In an interview, DeRosa spoke of her role as an Italian American writer. "Our grandparents and parents were bound to survival; we, on the other hand, have become freer to use our own talents and to rescue the talents of those who came before us. Because we have passed through more time, we have perspective that gives us the ability to look back and to judge their experiences as treasures that we cannot throw out."[32]

Another third-generation Italian American writer and scholar is Helen Barolini. Her first novel, *Umbertina* (1979), explores the lives of three women of the same family, each of whom is caught in the tangle of Old World and New World values.

Six years later, Barolini published *The Dream Book* (1985), an anthology of writing by fifty-five Italian American women, including Mary Gordon, Anne Attura Paolucci (who has written poetry, books of literary criticism, historical plays, essays, and short stories), and Barbara Grizzuti Harrison, known mostly for her essays, which have appeared in many magazines. Barolini's anthology contains the oral autobiography of Rosa Cassettari, as told to Marie Hall Etts in *Rosa: The Life of an Italian Immigrant* (1970). At the end of her life, the widowed Rosa says, "I have it like heaven now, no man to scold me and make me do this and stop me to do that ... I have it like heaven—I'm my own boss."

In her preface, Barolini writes, "Being Italian American, being female, and being a writer is being thrice an outsider, and why this is so is partly in the history and social background of the Italian women who came to this country, partly in the literary mold of the country itself."

Although they were outsiders, many Italian American women did go on to become well known. These women include Frances Xavier Cabrini, canonized in 1946; Anne Italiano, who became the film and stage star Anne Bancroft; singer Nancy Sinatra; Ella Grasso, the first woman to achieve the office of state governor (Connecticut); and Laura D'Andrea Tyson, the head of the Council of Economic Advisors for President Bill Clinton.

Italian American women have added their efforts and voices to those of other men and women in the United States, contributing in large and small ways to American culture and society.

---

[32] Mangione and Morreale, op. cit.

The stereotype of the all-powerful Italian mother was reinforced by this photo of baseball great Joe DiMaggio and his mother. DiMaggio had just joined the New York Yankees when this photo was taken in 1934.

A Few Famous Italian Americans

The list of accomplished Italian Americans is very long and new names are added each year. Some of the most famous Italian Americans include those in the film industry— Rudolph Valentino, Marilyn Monroe, Ida Lupino, Frank Capra, Michael Cimino, Al Pacino, Robert DeNiro, Francis Ford Coppola, and Martin Scorsese; and in the arts—the tenor Mario Lanza, the conductor Arturo Toscanini, and the singers Tony Bennett, Frank Sinatra, and Madonna. Italian Americans have been some of the nation's greatest athletes, such as Rocky Marciano, Mario Andretti, Joe Montana, Joe DiMaggio, Yogi Berra, and Phil Rizutto. Italian Americans have long been involved in U.S. politics, from the influential Filippo Mazzei to Rhode Island governor John Pastor, New York mayor Fiorello LaGuardia, former New York governor Mario Cuomo, and U.S. congresswoman Susan Molinari. Other famous figures include former Chrysler chairman Lee Iacocca and the president of the National Organization of Women, Eleanor Cutri Smeal.

Resources

HISTORY OF ITALY AND ITALIAN AMERICANS

American Italian Historical Association. *Perspectives in Italian Immigration and Ethnicity.* **New York: Center for Migration Studies, 1977.**

> Essays on ethnicity and social class from a symposium. Includes bibliographic references.

Amfitheatrof, Erik. *The Children of Columbus: An Informal History of the Italians in the New World.* **Boston: Little, Brown, 1973.**

> A study of the Italian immigrant experience in the United States, with emphasis on prominent Italians.

Barzini, Luigi. *From Caesar to the Mafia.* **London: H. Hamilton, 1971.**

> Illuminating sketches of Italian and Italian American life.

———. *O America, When You and I Were Young.* **Milan, Italy: A. Mondadori, 1978.**

> A journalist's reminiscences about his native and his adopted land.

Battistella, Graziano, ed. *Italian Americans in the '80s: A Sociodemographic Profile.* **New York: Center for Migration Studies, 1989.**

> Provides a variety of census data, including statistics from states with a high population of Italian Americans.

Bayor, Ronald. *Neighbors in Conflict: The Irish, Germans, Jews and Italians of New York City, 1929–1941.* **Baltimore: Johns Hopkins University Press, 1978.**

A multiethnic look at Italian and other recent immigrants in New York City before World War II, and the tensions among immigrant groups.

Briani, Vittorio. *Italian Immigrants Abroad: A Bibliography on the Italian Experience Outside Italy in Europe, the Americas, Australia, and Africa.* **Detroit: B. Ethridge Books, 1979.**

A comparative look at the Italian experience (primarily that of laborers) in America and elsewhere.

Briggs, John W. *An Italian Passage: Immigrants to Three American Cities, 1890–1930.* **New Haven: Yale University Press, 1978.**

Three case studies of immigrants in Rochester and Utica, New York, and Kansas City, Missouri, illustrating the commonalities and differences in the immigrant experience.

Brownstone, David M.; Franck, Irene; and Brownstone, Douglass L. *Island of Hope, Island of Tears.* **New York: Rawson, Wade Publishers, 1979.**

Provides a detailed account of the immigrant experience on Ellis Island.

Caso, Adolph. *Mass Media vs. the Italian Americans.* **Boston: Branden Press, 1980.**

This book deals with specific issues concerning the American way of life and the role played by Italian Americans.

Cateura, Linda Brandi. *Growing Up Italian.* **New York: William Morrow, 1987.**

This autobiography of an Italian American woman gives many insights into the trials and triumphs of women immigrants.

Child, Irvin L. *Italian or American? The Second Generation in Conflict.* **New York: Russell and Russell, 1943; reprint, 1970.**

A sociological study of the Italian American community in New Haven, Connecticut, focusing on the problems of acculturation. Bibliography.

Clark, Francis E. *Our Italian Fellow Citizens*. **Boston: Little, Brown, 1919.**

An early book recognizing the achievements of some Italian Americans.

Cordasco, Francesco. *The Italian-American Experience: An Annotated and Classified Bibliographical Guide*. **New York: B. Franklin, 1974.**

This bibliography contains 338 entries under the following categories: Bibliographies and Archives, Italian Emigration to America, Italian American History and Regional Studies, Sociology of Italian American Life, and Political and Economic Context of Italian American Life.

————. *Italian-Americans: A Guide to Information Sources*. **Detroit: Gale Research Co., 1978.**

References to books and periodicals under the following categories: General Reference Works, Social Sciences, Historical and Regional Studies, Applied Sciences, Humanities, Newpapers and Periodicals, and Fraternal, Professional and Religious Organizations. Includes title, subject, and author indexes.

Covello, Leonard. *The Social Background of the Italo-American School Child*. **Totowa, NJ: Rowman and Littlefield, 1972.**

The author, a well-known educator, studies the values of southern Italian families and their impact on the education of children, both in Italy and in the United States.

Covello, Leonard, with Guido D'Agostino. *The Heart Is the Teacher*. **New York: McGraw Hill, 1958.**

The autobiography of Covello.

Crawford, Francis Marion. *The Rulers of the South: Sicily, Calabria, Malta.* **London: Macmillan, 1900.**

A detailed history of the region from which the great majority of immigrants came.

D'Angelo, Pasquale. *Son of Italy.* **1924. Reprint, New York: Arno Press, 1975.**

The autobiography of an Italian immigrant who came to the United States in 1910 when he was sixteen, worked as a laborer, learned English, and eventually became a writer and poet.

DeConde, Alexander. *Half Bitter, Half Sweet: An Excursion into Italian-American History.* **New York: Scribner, 1971.**

This book, by a leading American diplomatic historian, emphasizes relations between the United States and Italy.

Di Franco, Philip. *The Italian American Experience.* **New York: Tor Books, 1988.**

A highly readable history of Italy and Italian Americans, from the ancient Etruscans through the rise and fall of Rome, the *Risorgimento,* and the great migration to the United States. The later chapters deal with famous Italian Americans in various fields.

Diggins, John P. *Mussolini and Fascism: The View from America.* **Princeton: Princeton University Press, 1972.**

An important book to read to gain a sense of the complicated feelings of Italian Americans toward the events and people of "the old country" during World War II.

Federal Writers' Project. *The Italians of New York.* **1938. Reprint, New York: Arno Press, 1969.**

A glimpse of the social life and customs of Italians living in New York in the 1930s. With photographs.

Fleming, Donald, and Bailyn, Bernard, eds. *The Intellectual Migration, Europe and America, 1930–1960.* Cambridge: Harvard University Press, 1969.

Collection of essays on the immigration of educated Italians and others.

Gambino, Richard. *Blood of My Blood: The Dilemma of the Italian-Americans.* New York: Doubleday, 1974.

The book weaves together history, sociology, and psychology to discuss the dilemmas of first-, second-, and third-generation Italian Americans. Includes many autobiographical tidbits.

———. *Vendetta.* Garden City, NY: Doubleday, 1977.

This book purports to tell "the true story of the worst lynching in America, the mass murder of Italian-Americans in New Orleans in 1891, the vicious motive behind it, and the tragic repercussions that continue to this day."

Garlick, Richard C., Jr., et al. *Italy and Italians in Washington's Time.* New York: Italian Publishers, 1933.

A look at some of the earliest Italian immigrants and their impact on the history of the United States.

Gisolfi, Anthony M. *Caudine Country: The Old World and an American Childhood.* New York: Senda Nueva de Ediciones, 1985.

A biography of the author's life in both Italy and America.

Gumina, Deanna Paoli. *The Italians in San Francisco, 1850–1890.* New York: Doubleday, 1978.

A look at the Italian immigrants who started their new lives in San Francisco.

Handlin, Oscar. *Boston's Immigrants: A Study in Acculturation.* Cambridge: Belknap Press of Harvard University Press, 1941, reprinted 1991.

A study of the social conditions and ethnic relations of Boston's immigrant communities, focusing especially on the conflicts between the Irish and Italian immigrants of Boston.

————. *The Uprooted*. **Boston: Little, Brown, 1973.**

Deals with the problems of and necessity for acculturation.

————. *This Was America: True Accounts of People and Places, Manners and Customs, as Recorded by European Travelers to the Western Shores in the 18th, 19th, and 20th Centuries*. **Cambridge: Harvard University Press, 1949.**

The subtitle of this book tells it all. Some especially interesting comments by Italians on their Italian American brethren.

Hansen, Marcus Lee. *The Immigrant in American History*. **Cambridge: Harvard University Press, 1940.**

Views of emigration and immigration in the middle of the twentieth century.

Heaps, William. *The Story of Ellis Island*. **New York: Seabury Press, 1967.**

An overview of the role of Ellis Island in immigration.

Hibbert, Christopher. *Garibaldi and His Enemies: The Clash of Arms and Personalities in the Making of Italy*. **Boston: Little, Brown, 1966.**

The book to read if you want to understand the many people and forces that eventually led to a united Italy.

Higham, John. *Strangers in the Land: Patterns of American Nativism 1860–1925*. **Westport, CT: Greenwood Press, 1980.**

Deals with the prejudices suffered by ethnic minorities. Nativism refers to a policy of favoring native inhabitants over immigrants.

————, ed. *Ethnic Leadership in America*. Baltimore: Johns Hopkins University Press, 1978.

> Papers from a symposium about ethnic Americans in leadership roles.

Hobbie, Margaret, compiler. *Italian-American Material Culture: A Directory of Collections, Sites, and Festivals in the United States and Canada*. Westport, CT: Greenwood Press, 1992.

> Locates and describes ethnic material culture and photo collections. Chapter 1 describes objects, photo images, and oral histories held by museums and other repositories; Chapter 2 lists examples of churches, houses, wineries, neighborhoods, and other sites associated with Italian American history; Chapter 3 describes more than one hundred religious feasts and secular festivals and foods.

Hoobler, Dorothy, and Hoobler, Thomas. *The Italian American Family Album*. New York: Oxford University Press, 1994.

> The story of Italian immigration is brought vividly to life with many excerpts from diaries, letters, newspapers, and interviews. It covers the old country, the journey to America, the life the immigrants made for themselves, and the contributions of Italian Americans, from the famous to the unknown. Contains many photographs and other scrapbook memorabilia.

Hutchinson, Edward Prince. *The Legislative History of American Immigration Policy 1798–1965*. Philadelphia: University of Pennsylvania Press, 1981.

> Includes statistics on the numbers of Italian immigrants in various years.

Iamurri, Gabriel A. *The True Story of an Immigrant*, rev. ed. Boston: Christopher, 1951.

Iamurri's perceptive and critical memoirs document his early life in Italy and his eagerness to see the world. His descriptions of immigrant processing and his first few months in the United States are very evocative of the immigrant experience.

Iorizzo, Luciano, and Mondello, Salvatore. *The Italian Americans*, **rev. ed. Boston: Twayne, 1980.**

A thorough study of the Italian immigrant experience in the United States. The book brings history and culture alive with many specific examples. It surveys Italian immigrants in farms, towns, and cities, addressing problems of crime and unfair labor practices. Includes a who's who of famous Italian Americans.

Johnson, Colleen Leahy. *Growing Up and Growing Old in Italian-American Families.* **New Brunswick: Rutgers University Press, 1988.**

A look at the difficulties facing Italian Americans as older adults. This book may give you insights that will help you prepare for interviews with elderly relatives.

Kennedy, John F. *A Nation of Immigrants*, **rev. ed. New York: Harper and Row, 1964.**

President Kennedy's book about our immigrant heritage, including sections on government immigration policy.

Kessner, Thomas. *The Golden Door: Italian and Jewish Immigrant Mobility in New York City, 1880–1915.* **New York: Oxford University Press, 1977.**

A look at the second, third, and fourth generations of urban immigrants and their upward mobility. The author contrasts the greater upward mobility of Jewish immigrants with that of Italian immigrants and explores the reasons for the difference.

———. *Fiorello H. LaGuardia and the Making of Modern New York.* **New York: McGraw-Hill, 1989.**

An illustrated biography of New York's first Italian American mayor.

Kessner, Thomas, and Caroli, Betty Boyd. *Today's Immigrants: Their Stories.* **New York: Oxford University Press, 1982.**

A look at the newest immigrants, including Italian immigrants in the latter part of the twentieth century.

Krause, Corinne Azen. *Grandmothers, Mothers, and Daughters.* **Boston: Twayne, 1991.**

Interviews with three generations of ethnic American women, including Italian American women.

LaGumina, Salvatore J. *WOP: A Documentary History of Anti-Italian Discrimination in the United States.* **San Francisco: Straight Arrow Books, 1973.**

A detailed examination of prejudice in Italian American history.

LaGumina, Salvatore J., ed. *Ethnicity in American Political Life: The Italian Experience.* **New York: American Italian Historical Association, 1968.**

Selected proceedings of a symposium on Italian Americans in politics.

La Sorte, Michael. *La Merica: Images of Italian Greenhorn Experience.* **Philadelphia: Temple University Press, 1985.**

The author draws on statistical documents and recent scholarly commentary, but concentrates on individual stories in published and unpublished diaries, letters, and autobiographies of the immigrants who lived the "greenhorn" experience.

LoPreato, Joseph. *Italian Americans.* **New York: Random House, 1970.**

This book covers the promise and problems of immigration, with insights into the forces that led thousands to leave southern Italy.

Lourdeaux, Lee. *Italian and Irish Filmmakers in America*. **Philadelphia: Temple University Press, 1990.**

A critical study of how these two immigrant groups have contributed to American cinema.

Mangano, Antonio. *Sons of Italy: A Social and Religious Study of the Italians in America*. **Boston: Little, Brown, 1917.**

An early study of Italian Americans that deals with the first concentrations of Italians in American cities and their assimilation.

Mangione, Jerre. *An Ethnic at Large*. **New York: Putnam, 1978.**

The author remembers his ethnic childhood in the 1930s and 1940s.

———. *America Is Also Italian*. **New York: G.P. Putnam's Sons, 1969.**

The impact of Italians and Italian Americans on U.S. history.

Mangione, Jerre, and Morreale, Ben. *La Storia*. **New York: HarperCollins, 1992.**

Detailed history of Italian American immigration, with background information on Italian unification. Includes a discussion of prominent Italian Americans in politics, sports, and other fields.

Marinacci, Barbara. *They Came from Italy*. **New York: Dodd, Mead and Co., 1967.**

The story of the Italian immigrants.

Marchelolo, Maurice R. *Black Coal for White Bread: Up from the Prairie Mines*. **New York: Vantage, 1972.**

An autobiographical account of the hard life of an immigrant miner.

Mariano, John Horace. *The Italian Contribution to American Democracy.* **Boston: Christopher Publishing House, 1921. Reprinted by Arno Press in 1975.**

Details the social and economic conditions of second-generation Italians in New York.

McFadden, Elizabeth. *The Glitter and the Gold.* **New York: Dial Press, 1971.**

An account of Luigi Palma Di Cesnola, the first director of the Metropolitan Museum of Art in New York.

Militello, Pietro. *Italians in America.* **Philadelphia: Franklin Publishing Co., 1973.**

A small book that details the lives of Italian Americans in Philadelphia.

Moquin, Wayne, and Van Doren, Charles, eds., with Francis A. J. Ianni, consulting ed. *A Documentary History of the Italian-Americans.* **New York: Praeger, 1974.**

The topics covered include the immigrant experience in Boston, California, New York, and Chicago; the jobs immigrants took; the problems of *padroni*, crime, and violence; and the emergence of the Italian American identity. Many primary sources make this a fascinating book.

Moquin, Wayne, and Van Doren, Charles, eds. *The American Way of Crime: A Documentary History.* **New York: Praeger, 1976.**

Details the history of organized crime in America, including the Mafia.

Morrison, Joan, and Zabusky, Charlotte Fox, eds. *American Mosaic: The Immigrant Experience in the Words of Those Who Lived It.* **New York: Dutton, 1980.**

This is a sweeping work that presents all strands of the immigrant experience of twentieth-century America. A number of the voices are Italian American.

Musmanno, Michael A. *The Story of Italians in America.* **Garden City, NY: Doubleday, 1965.**

An overview of Italians in America, from Christopher Columbus to famous Italian Americans of modern times.

Neidle, Cecyle S. *America's Immigrant Women.* **Boston: Twayne Publishers, 1975.**

Biographies of immigrant women and their daughters.

Nelli, Humbert S. *Italians in Chicago, 1880–1930.* **New York: Oxford University Press, 1970.**

An especially useful book if your immigrant ancestors settled in Chicago's large Italian American community.

————. *From Immigrants to Ethnics: The Italian Americans.* **Oxford, U.K.: Oxford University Press, 1983.**

A fine historical overview of the Italian experience in the United States from Christopher Columbus to Francis Ford Coppola. Includes discussion of the different experiences of Italian Americans in eastern, midwestern, and western cities.

———— ed. *The United States and Italy: The First Two Hundred Years.* **Staten Island, NY: American Italian Historical Association, 1977.**

A collection of essays on Italian emigration and immigrants in the United States.

Null, Gary, and Stone, Carl. *The Italian Americans.* **Harrisburg, PA: Stackpole Books, 1976.**

Minibiographies of eminent Italians and Italian Americans from Columbus to Frank Zappa.

Panella, Vincent. *The Other Side: Growing Up Italian in America.* **Garden City, NY: Doubleday, 1979.**

An engaging and insightful account of the author's experiences.

Panunzio, Constantine Maria. *Soul of an Immigrant.* **New York: Macmillan, 1921.**

In his autobiography, Panunzio depicts his often demeaning and harsh experiences as an immigrant at age nineteen in 1902. Panunzio worked at various laborer jobs, learned English, and became a preacher, a teacher, and eventually a professor of sociology at the University of California.

Pellegrini, Angelo. *American Dream: An Immigrant's Quest.* **San Francisco: North Point Press, 1986.**

The autobiographical narrative of an Italian immigrant, focusing on his "gradual discovery of America and of himself in relation to his adopted country."

———. *Americans by Choice.* **New York: Macmillan, 1956.**

Oral history and biography of some representative first-generation Italian Americans. The cast includes La Bimbina, a peasant mother; Louis Martini, a winegrower; Rosa Mondavi, mother to winegrowers; Guido Sella, a bootlegger; Celestino, "a roving parasite"; Leonardo, a ditchdigger, and Angelo Pellegrini, the narrator.

Pisani, Lawrence Frank. *The Italian in America: A Social Study and History.* **New York: Exposition Press, 1957.**

Another good social history that seeks to "illustrate how the interplay of peoples and cultures contributes to the development and strength of the U.S."

Pitkin, Thomas, and Cordasco, Francesco. *The Black Hand: A Chapter in Ethnic Crime.* **Totowa, NJ: Littlefield, Adams, 1977.**

A history of the Black Hand, a much feared secret society, and the role of Italian Americans in organized crime.

Preston, William, Jr. *Aliens and Dissenters: Federal Suppression of Radicals, 1903–1933.* **Urbana: University of Illinois Press, 1994.**

A history of the U.S. government's response to radicals of many ethnicities, including many Italian American labor leaders.

Rips, Gladys Nadler. *Coming to America: Immigrants from Southern Europe.* **New York: Delacorte Press, 1983.**

Includes a lengthy section on Italian immigrants.

Rolle, Andrew. *The Italian Americans: Troubled Roots.* **Norman: University of Oklahoma Press, 1980.**

The author seeks to interpret the confusion felt by Italian immigrants in the United States and "to fuse psychoanalysis with history." Includes vivid biographical sketches of Rudolph Valentino, Frank Sinatra, Fiorello LaGuardia, Al Capone, and others.

———. *The Immigrant Upraised: Italian Adventurers and Colonists in an Expanding America.* **Norman: University of Oklahoma Press, 1968.**

A thorough study of the contributions of Italian immigrants, their role in settling the frontier, and the problems of assimilation.

Russell, Francis. *Tragedy in Dedham.* **New York: McGraw Hill, 1962.**

An account of the Sacco-Vanzetti trial in Massachusetts.

Sartorio, Henry Charles. *Social and Religious Life of Italians in America.* **Boston, 1918. Reprint, Clifton NJ: A. M. Kelley, 1974.**

An early look at the newest group of immigrants of the time.

Saveth, Edward N. *American Historians and European Immigrants, 1875–1925*. **New York: Russell and Russell, 1948, reprinted 1965.**

A historiography of the time period that included the great wave of Italian immigrants.

Scarpaci, Vincenza. *A Portrait of the Italians in America*. **New York: Scribner, 1982.**

An informal view of how Italian immigrants have adapted to their new homeland.

Schiavo, Giovanni E. *Four Centuries of Italian-American History*. **New York: Vigo Press, 1954.**

One of the definitive histories of Italian Americans. For an in-depth examination of the history of Italian Americans in a certain time period or place, see Schiavo's books below.

———. *Italian-American History*. **2 vols. New York: Vigo Press, 1947–1949.**

———. *The Italians in America Before the Revolution*. **New York: Vigo Press, 1976.**

———. *The Italians in America Before the Civil War*. **New York: Vigo Press, 1934.**

———. *The Italians in Chicago*. **Chicago: University of Chicago Press, 1928.**

———. *The Italians in Missouri*. **New York: Arno Press, 1975.**

Schoener, Allon. *The Italian Americans*. **New York: Macmillan, 1987.**

A good introduction to the history of Italian Americans.

Sennet, Richard, and Cobb, Jonathan. *The Hidden Injuries of Class*. **New York: Knopf, 1993.**

A sociological study of immigrant alienation because of conflicts of social class.

Talese, Gay. *Unto the Sons*. **New York: Knopf, 1992.**

The immigrant saga is brought close to home through the lives of the author's forebears, particularly his Italian-born father. The book is a compelling genealogical tale, interweaving historic fact with the lore the author has gathered from family tales, interviews, letters, and diaries.

Taylor, David A., and Williams, John Alexander, eds. *Old Ties, New Attachments: Italian-American Folklife in the West*. **Washington, DC: Library of Congress, 1992.**

Details the lives of Italian immigrants and their descendants who made their home in the western United States.

Tomasi, Lydio F. *The Italian American Family*. **New York: Center for Migration Studies, 1972.**

Examines the adjustments families from southern Italy had to make to cope with life in urban America.

———. *The Italian Immigrant Woman in North America*. **New York: Proceedings of the American Italian Historical Society, 1978.**

A paper dealing with the unique situation of Italian American women in the United States.

Tomasi, Silvano, and Engels, Madeline, eds. *The Italian Experience in the United States*. **New York: Center for Migration Studies, 1970.**

Ten articles on various aspects of the Italian American experience in the United States.

Ventresca, Francesco. *Personal Reminiscences of a Naturalized American*. **New York: Rueson, 1937.**

Autobiographical narrative instilled with the author's high

hopes and optimism. It is based on a diary that Ventresca kept during the first years after his arrival in 1908.

Wechman, Robert J. *The Economic Development of the Italian American*. **Champaign, IL: Stipes Publishing Co., 1983.**

Includes the contribution of Italian mutual benefit organizations to the economic development of immigrants.

Whyte, William Foote. *Street Corner Society: The Social Structure of an Italian Slum*, **4th ed. Chicago: University of Chicago Press, 1993.**

Italian American gangs in Chicago in the early part of the century.

ORGANIZED CRIME

Albini, Joseph L. *The American Mafia*. **New York: Appleton Century Crofts, 1971.**

An overview of the history of the American Mafia, offshoot of the criminal secret society that originated in Sicily.

Lewis, Norman. *The Honored Society: The Sicilian Mafia Observed*. **New York: Hippocrene Books, 1984.**

The origins and development of the Sicilian Mafia.

ITALIAN AMERICAN WOMEN

Anderson, Christopher P. *Madonna, Unauthorized*. **New York: Simon & Schuster, 1991.**

An unauthorized biography of the singer and actor.

Barolini, Helen, ed. *The Dream Book*. **New York: Schocken Books, 1985.**

This book contains the work of fifty-five Italian American women writers and an excellent introduction by the editor. Barolini explains that she put this anthology together to answer the question, "Where are the women?" The editor also addresses the seeds of doubt that are internal blocks to so many creative and talented Italian American women.

Breslin, Rosemary. *Gerry: A Woman Making History.* **New York: Pinnacle Books, 1984.**

A biography of Geraldine Ferraro, with photographs from the 1984 presidential campaign.

Capozzoli, Mary Jane. *Three Generations of Italian American Women in Nassau County, 1925–81.* **New York: Garland, 1990.**

A close look at the lives of first-, second-, and third-generation Italian American women.

Caroli, Betty Boyd; Harney, Robert F.; and Tomasi, Lydio F., eds. *The Italian Immigrant Woman in North America.* **Toronto: Multicultural History Society of Ontario, 1978.**

A collection of essays on women immigrants.

Cohen, Miriam. *Workshop to Office: Two Generations of Italian Women in New York City, 1900–1950.* **Ithaca, NY: Cornell University Press, 1992.**

This book details the lives of Italian American women in New York during the first half of the twentieth century.

Cordasco, Francesco. *The Immigrant Woman in North America: An Annotated Bibliography of Selected References.* **Metuchen, NJ: Scarecrow Press, 1985.**

This bibliography is a good place to start if you want to find out more about the female immigrant experience.

Corte, Robert. *They Made It in America: A Celebration of the Achievements of Great Italian Americans.* **New York: Morrow and Co., 1993.**

A series of minibiographies of the most famous Italian Americans.

Etts, Marie Hall. *Rosa: The Life of an Italian Immigrant*. St. Paul: University of Minnesota Press, 1970.

The oral autobiography of an Italian immigrant woman, as told to Marie Etts.

Ewen, Elizabeth. *Immigrant Women in the Land of Dollars*. New York: Monthly Review Press, 1985.

The stories of immigrant women in the United States, many of whom took jobs in industry for the first time in their lives.

Ferraro, Geraldine, and Francke, Linda Bird. *Ferraro, My Story*. New York: Bantam Books, 1985.

An autobiography with a focus on the 1984 presidential campaign.

Harrison, Barbara Grizzuti. *Italian Days*. New York: Weidenfeld and Nicolson, 1989.

A book of description and travel with many reminiscences by the author.

Maglione, Connie A., and Fiore, Carmen Anthony. *Voices of the Daughters*. Princeton, NJ: Townhouse Publishing, 1989.

A compilation of the thoughts, feelings, attitudes, and interests of Italian American women, spanning all ages and geographic areas of the United States.

Odencrantz, Louise. *Italian Women in Industry*. Fairfield, NJ: Augustus M. Kelley Publishers, 1976.

A detailed study of the jobs Italian women took when they came to the United States.

Tomasi, Lydio F., and Caroli, Betty Boyd. *The Italian Immigrant Woman in North America*. New York:

American Italian Historical Association, 1979.

Another comprehensive look at the lives of Italian immigrant women.

Torgovnick, Marianna. *Crossing Ocean Parkway: Readings by an Italian American Daughter.* **Chicago: University of Chicago Press, 1994.**

This memoir combines American literature, history, and criticism with the author's own autobiography, focusing on her life in the Italian American community of New York.

Vermilye, Jerry. *Ida Lupino.* **New York: Pyramid Publications, 1977.**

A biography of the Italian American actress and director.

ITALIAN AMERICAN NOVELISTS

Green, Rose Basile. *The Italian-American Novel: A Document of the Interaction of Two Cultures.* **Rutherford, NJ: Fairleigh Dickinson University Press, 1974.**

A comprehensive study of significant contributions made by Italian American novelists.

Peragallo, Olga. *Italian-American Authors and Their Contribution to American Literature.* **New York: S. V. Vanni, 1949.**

The important Italian American authors at the midpoint of the twentieth century.

NOVELS

Angelo, Valenti. *The Golden Gate.* **New York: Viking Press, 1939, reprint Arno Press, 1975.**

A literary chronicle describing the early years of an immigrant boy, "Nino," as he settles in his new country. Other novels by Angelo include: *The Hill of Little Miracles,*

1942; *The Rooster Club*, 1944; and *Bells of Bleecker Street*, 1949.

Arleo, Joseph. *The Grand Street Collector.* **New York: Walker, 1970.**

Fictional account of the political assassination of an exiled Italian political leader in New York City during World War II.

Barolini, Antonio. *Our Last Family Countess and Related Stories.* **New York: Harper, 1956.**

Short stories about an Italian immigrant.

Basso, Hamilton. *Days Before Lent.* **New York: Scribner, 1939.**

Novel about Italian Americans in New Orleans.

Benesutti, Marion. *No Steady Job for Papa.* **New York: Vanguard, 1966.**

Novel about southern Italian immigrant life in the Italian neighborhood of Philadelphia.

Calitri, Charles. *Father.* **New York: Crown, 1962.**

An intricately plotted novel about an Italian immigrant priest, his emigration to the United States, and his eventual disengagement from the Roman Catholic Church.

Canzoneri, Robert. *A Highly Ramified Tree.* **New York: Viking, 1976.**

An Italian American poet and teacher searches for meaning by tracing his Sicilian immigrant father's life in Sicily and Mississippi.

Corsel, Ralph. *Up There the Stars.* **New York: Citadel, 1968.**

Novel about Italian immigrant life in New York City, with themes of ethnic conflict and acculturation.

D'Agostino, Guido. *Olives on the Apple Tree.* **New York: Doubleday, Doran, 1940.**

A richly textured novel of Italian immigrant life in the United States that deals with isolation, conflict, and acculturation.

D'Angelo, Lou. *What the Ancients Said.* **New York: Doubleday, 1971.**

Novel set in New York City in the 1940s, dealing with the Americanization of Italian immigrants.

D'Angelo, Pascal. *Son of Italy.* **New York: Macmillan, 1924. Reprint, New York: Arno Press, 1975.**

Autobiographical narrative of an Italian immigrant who arrived in 1910 and worked as a day laborer.

De Capite, Michael. *Maria.* **New York: John Day, 1943.**

Novel about three generations in the life of an Italian American family in Cleveland in the 1920s.

De Capite, Raymond. *The Coming of Fabrizze.* **New York: McKay, 1960.**

A story of Italian immigrant life in the Midwest.

Di Donato, Pietro. *Christ in Concrete.* **Indianapolis: Bobbs-Merrill, 1939.**

Autobiographical first novel about the world of Italian immigrants, their hardships and successes.

———. *Naked Author.* **New York: Phaedre, 1970.**

Collection of short stories about Italian Americans.

———. *Three Circles of Light.* **New York: Messner, 1960.**

Novel of immigrant life set in the slums of West Hoboken, New Jersey.

Fante, John. *Dago Red.* **New York: Viking, 1940.**

Sketches of Italian Americans in a small town near Denver as seen through the eyes of a small boy.

————. *The Brotherhood of the Grape*. **New York: Houghton Mifflin, 1977.**

A raucous yet tender novel of Italian American life set in the San Joaquin Valley of California.

————. *Wait Until Spring, Bandini*. **New York: Stackpole, 1938.**

Novel set in Colorado about an Italian laborer and his family.

————. *Ask the Dust*. **New York: Stackpole, 1939.**

The saga of an aspiring Italian American writer in Los Angeles.

Forgione, Louis. *The River Between*. **New York: E.P. Dutton, 1928. Reprint, New York: Arno Press, 1975.**

A realistic novel about the Italian American experience.

Fumento, Rocco. *Tree of Dark Reflection*. **New York: Knopf, 1962.**

The story of an Italian immigrant in Massachusetts.

Gallico, Paul. *The Small Miracle*. **Garden City, NY: Doubleday, 1952.**

A charming novel about a boy who asks St. Francis and the pope to help cure his ill donkey.

Lapolla, Garibaldi Marto. *The Fire in the Flesh*. **New York: Vanguard Press, 1931. Reprint, New York: Arno Press, 1975.**

This novel and Lapolla's *The Grand Gennaro* (Vanguard, 1935) are panoramic portraits of the Italian community in New York City.

Malanga, Gerard. *Incarnations*. **Los Angeles: Black Sparrow Press, 1974.**

A book of poems with references to the Italian American situation.

Mangione, Jerre. *Mount Allegro*. Boston: Houghton Mifflin, 1943.

A collection of interconnected stories about Sicilian immigrants living in Rochester, New York.

———. *Reunion in Sicily*. Boston: Houghton Mifflin, 1950.

The author returns to the land of his ancestors and writes a book that is part travelogue, part autobiography.

Mirabelli, Eugene. *The Burning Air*. Boston: Houghton Mifflin, 1959.

Novel of second-generation Italian Americans and the problems of assimilation.

Pagano, John. *Golden Wedding*. New York: Random House, 1943. Reprint, New York: Arno Press, 1975.

The story of an Italian family's voyage to the United States and their life in Colorado, Utah, and California.

———. *The Paesanos*. Boston: Little Brown, 1940.

A collection of humorous stories about Italian immigrants in Los Angeles.

Panetta, George. *We Ride a White Donkey*. New York: Harcourt Brace, 1944.

Vignettes of Italian American life on Mulberry Street, New York City.

Papaleo, Joseph. *Out of Place*. Boston: Little Brown, 1970.

The theme of this novel is the protagonist's rejection of the American environment and his return to Italy to discover his identity.

Pei, Mario. *The Sparrows of Paris.* **New York: Random House, 1958.**

A detective story involving the supernatural, narcotics traffickers, and political terrorists.

Puzo, Mario. *The Godfather.* **New York: Putnam, 1969.**

The story of Don Vito Corleone, his family, the immigrant experience, and the Mafia. For mature readers.

———. *The Fortunate Pilgrim.* **London: Heinemann, 1965.**

The story of an Italian immigrant in New York in the 1930s.

Talese, Gay. *Honor Thy Father.* **New York: World Publishers, 1971.**

Novel about the Mafia. For mature readers.

Tomasi, Mari. *Like Lesser Gods.* **Milwaukee: Bruce Publishers, 1949.**

Novel about Italian workers in the granite quarries of Vermont, their folkways, and the merging of two cultures.

Vergara, Joe. *Love and Pasta.* **New York: Harper and Row, 1969.**

A panoramic novel centering on an Italian American's divided allegiance in World War II.

FILMS

The Godfather (1972).

Director, Francis Ford Coppola. Adaptation of Mario Puzo's novel about the Mafia. Marlon Brando, Al Pacino, and James Caan. For mature audiences.

The Godfather, Part II (1974).

Sequel starring Al Pacino, Diane Keaton, Robert DeNiro,

and Talia Shire. For mature audiences.

The Godfather, Part III (1990).

Directed by Coppola. For mature audiences.

Goodfellas (1990).

Directed by Martin Scorsese. The daily life of a hood and his rise in the Mafia. Starring Robert DeNiro, Ray Liotta, Lorraine Bracco, and Joe Pesci. For mature audiences.

Little Caesar (1930).

Directed by Mervyn LeRoy, this hard-hitting gangster film stars Edward G. Robinson and Douglas Fairbanks, Jr.

Love Story (1970).

Directed by Arthur Miller and stars Ali MacGraw, Ryan O'Neal, and Ray Milland.

Marty (1955).

Directed by Delbert Mann from a script by Paddy Chayefsky. Stars Ernest Borgnine, who won an Oscar for his performance, and Betsy Blair.

Mean Streets (1973).

Directed by Martin Scorsese and featuring Robert DeNiro and Harvey Keitel, the movie recreates the atmosphere of New York's Little Italy. For mature audiences.

Rocky (1976).

Directed by John Avildsen. This first of the Rocky films catapulted actor Sylvester Stallone into the movie big leagues.

The Rose Tattoo (1955).

Daniel Mann directed this film adaptation of Tennessee Williams's play about a Sicilian widow who is obsessed by her dead husband until a Sicilian truck driver enters her life. It stars Anna Magnani and Burt Lancaster.

Serpico (1973).

Directed by Sidney Lumet. A galvanizing adaptation of the Peter Maas book about an undercover cop, played with high energy by Al Pacino. For mature audiences.

Somebody up There Likes Me (1956).

Directed by Robert Wise and starring Paul Newman and Sal Mineo, a fictionalized account of the life of the boxer Rocky Graziano.

Wise Guys (1986).

Directed by Brian DePalma and starring Danny DeVito, Harvey Keitel, and Ray Sharkey. For mature audiences.

1900 (1977).

Directed by Bernardo Bertolucci. A five-hour epic that chronicles the history, politics, and social changes of a small Italian province from 1900 until the defeat of Mussolini in 1945. Starring Burt Lancaster, Robert DeNiro, and a large international cast. For mature audiences.

EDUCATIONAL FILMS

Ave Maria: The Story of the Fisherman's Feast (1956).

Documentary on Boston's annual Festa del Madonna del Soccoroso.

Dreams of Distant Shores (1987).

Documentary about European immigrants to the United States and Canada during the period 1890–1915.

Hello, Columbus! (1988).

Documentary on the celebration of Columbus Day in San Francisco.

Journey to Freedom (1986).

Documentary of nineteenth-century immigrants who settled in the eastern United States.

The New Pilgrims (1987).

Study of the effect of immigrants on North American society.

When You Make a Good Crop: Italians in the Delta (1988).

Study of the Italian American traditions in the Delta region of the Mississippi River.

FAMOUS ITALIANS AND ITALIAN AMERICANS

Cuomo, Mario. *The New York Idea: An Experiment in Democracy*. New York: Crown, 1994.

The views of the former governor of New York on economic, social, and public policy.

D'Amato, Al. *Power, Pasts, and Politics: The World According to Senator Al D'Amato*. New York: Hyperion, 1995.

The autobiography of the colorful and outspoken grandson of immigrants who became the first Italian American senator from New York.

Fermi, Laura. *Mussolini*. Chicago and London: University of Chicago Press, 1961.

The author and her husband, the physicist Enrico Fermi, fled Italy when Mussolini began implementing anti-Jewish laws. This book is her account of Mussolini and his time.

Gallagher, Dorothy. *All the Right Enemies: The Murder of Carlo Tresca*. New Brunswick, NJ: Rutgers University Press, 1988.

The life and times of the labor leader Carlo Tresca.

La Guardia, Fiorello. *Fiorello H. LaGuardia. The*

Making of an Insurgent. New York: Capricorn Books, 1961.

LaGuardia's very readable autobiography.

Mack Smith, Denis. *Cavour*. **New York: Alfred A. Knopf, 1985.**

A good biography of one of the main players in the unification of Italy.

————. *Mussolini*. **London: Paladin/Granada, 1983.**

A comprehensive biography of the leader of fascist Italy.

Mann, Arthur. *LaGuardia: A Fighter Against His Times, 1882–1933*. **New York: J.B. Lippincott Company, 1959.**

A lively biography of New York's first Italian American mayor.

Marchione, Margherita. *Philip Mazzei: Jefferson's Zealous Whig*. **New York: American Institute of Italian Studies, n.d.**

A biography of the Italian who had a great impact on the writing of the Declaration of Independence.

Vanzetti, Francesco. *Personal Reminiscences of a Naturalized American*. **New York: Rueson, 1937.**

A powerful autobiographical account of an immigrant's life and imprisonment.

ITALIAN AMERICAN SOCIETIES

America-Italy Society
38 East 57th Street
New York, NY 10022

Founded: 1949. Members: 1,400. The society promotes appreciation of the cultural heritage and contributions of

Italy. It sponsors cultural exchanges, tours, workshops, and Italian language classes.

American-Italian Congress
111 Columbia Heights
Brooklyn, NY 11201

This federation of organizations supports the greater appreciation of contributions made by Italian Americans to American political, social, cultural, and economic life. The federation makes grants to college students, sponsors essay contests, and maintains a research library with a great deal of biographical information. It also maintains the Italian Hall of Fame.

Americans of Italian Descent
51 Madison Avenue
New York, NY 10010

Founded: 1965. Members: 30,000. A civil rights organization dedicated to fighting discrimination against Americans of Italian descent.

Italian-American Cultural Society
2811 Imperial Avenue
Warren, MI 48093

Founded: 1957. Members: 2,500. Encourages appreciation of the contributions Italy and Italians have made to the United States and Canada. Offers awards to stress the importance of Italian cultural achievements.

National Italian-American Foundation
666 11th Street NW
Washington, DC 20001

A government liaison and lobbying organization designed to advance the interests of Italian Americans. Provides information services and a speakers' bureau, as well as grants and scholarships to those doing studies in areas of interest to Italian Americans.

MUSEUMS

City Lore (The New York Center for Urban Folk Culture)
72 East First Street
New York, NY 10003

This museum is open by appointment only. It has a large photo collection and oral history collection, including materials on Italian American immigrants.

Ellis Island Immigration Museum
U.S. Department of the Interior
National Park Service
New York, NY 10004

Over 3 million Italian and Sicilian immigrants passed through Ellis Island, so there is a good chance that one of your ancestors did. The museum is a beautiful and moving collection of photographs and artifacts, including textiles, rosaries, toys, dolls, clothes, and musical instruments. There is also a movie presentation of the history of Ellis Island.

Lower East Side Tenement Museum
97 Orchard Street
New York, NY 10002

This museum specializes in "living history," including dramatizations and walking tours. Part of the museum is a recreation of an Italian tenement of the 1930s.

Chapter 3
Beginning Your Genealogical Search

In the last chapter you read about when, why, and how many Italians immigrated to the United States. In those pages you also read excerpts of their stories, told in their own words. Now it is time for you to begin gathering the information that will allow you to tell your own story. The remaining chapters of this book will describe the tools you need, methods to use, and the different ways you can record your own family's history.

Genealogical research is similar to the work of a detective. A detective tries to discover who did what, when, where, how, and why. As you delve into your family history, you'll discover answers to questions such as: Which of your ancestors left Italy to come to the United States? Why did they decide to come to the United States? Did they leave from the Sicilian port of Palermo, or the main Italian ports of Genoa or Naples? Did they suffer through the long journey in steerage? Or did an earlier immigrant send them enough money to travel in first or second class? Did your ancestors land at New York, Boston, or New Orleans? Did they pass through Ellis Island? Did they stay and work in the city they first entered, or travel on to other cities or rural areas? Whom did they marry? How many children did they have? What kind of work did they do? Were any of them anything like you in personality or physical appearance? In your research you will discover answers to these and many other questions. You may even discover things about yourself—the origin of your lefthandedness, for example, or the source of your musical talent.

Your genealogical research will be a way not only of discovering the past, but of preserving it. The end product of

One of the goals of your search might be to determine your ancestor's point of entry. During its years of operation, approximately one-third of the immigrants who passed through Ellis Island were Italian.

your research—whether it is a family tree, a family history book complete with photographs and memorabilia, or a taped set of oral history interviews with relatives—will be a lasting legacy for your relatives and future descendants, as well as for your community and future researchers.

Getting Organized

In genealogical research, as in many other activities, it is a good idea to get organized before jumping into the task. A number of ready-made organizing systems are available through genealogical associations, including computer software systems (see the **Resources** at the end of this chapter). You can use one of these or gradually develop your own system. Whatever you choose, you'll find that your genealogical work will proceed faster and more smoothly if you organize your information. The more systematic your charts and notes are, the more clearly you'll be able to see what you know and what you still need to find out.

An Italian American Photo Album

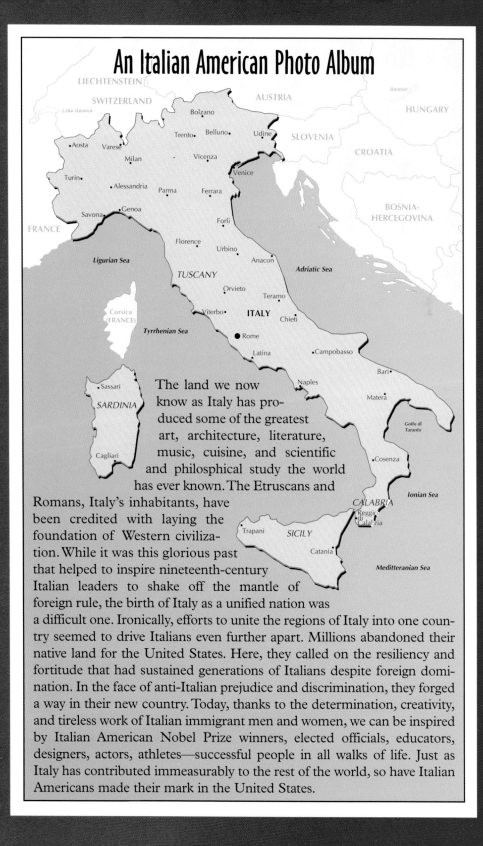

The land we now know as Italy has produced some of the greatest art, architecture, literature, music, cuisine, and scientific and philosphical study the world has ever known. The Etruscans and Romans, Italy's inhabitants, have been credited with laying the foundation of Western civilization. While it was this glorious past that helped to inspire nineteenth-century Italian leaders to shake off the mantle of foreign rule, the birth of Italy as a unified nation was a difficult one. Ironically, efforts to unite the regions of Italy into one country seemed to drive Italians even further apart. Millions abandoned their native land for the United States. Here, they called on the resiliency and fortitude that had sustained generations of Italians despite foreign domination. In the face of anti-Italian prejudice and discrimination, they forged a way in their new country. Today, thanks to the determination, creativity, and tireless work of Italian immigrant men and women, we can be inspired by Italian American Nobel Prize winners, elected officials, educators, designers, actors, athletes—successful people in all walks of life. Just as Italy has contributed immeasurably to the rest of the world, so have Italian Americans made their mark in the United States.

The Forum was the administrative and corporate center of ancient Rome. The Forum contained temples, a basilica that served as a hall of justice and public meeting place, a speakers' platform, and several triumphal arches. The building of the Forum took place under the reign of numerous Roman emperors and stretched from the sixth century BC to the beginning of the seventh century AD.

The city of Venice is famous for its canals, architecture, art museums, palaces, and churches. Venice was one of Europe's most powerful city-states in the fourteenth, fifteenth, and sixteenth centuries, controlling commerce between Asia and Europe and dominating the seas.

Italy is a diverse country, with each region boasting its own unique history, culture, foods, and art forms. The city of Orvieto is located in the Umbria region of central Italy. It was once an independent Etruscan city-state.

Located off the southwest coast of Italy is the island of Sicily, which is surrounded by the Mediterranean, Ionian, and Tyrrhenian Seas. Sicily is a large producer of olives, grapes for wine, and other fruits and vegetables. In port towns like Sciacca, pictured above, fishing for tuna and other types of fish is a major source of income.

Far from Sicily lies the northern Italian region of South Tyrol, dominated by the Alps and bordering Austria. South Tyrol, which contains both Italian-speaking and German-speaking areas, became part of the Italian political region of Trentino-Alto-Adige in 1919.

Raphael, shown above in a self-portrait, was one of Renaissance Rome's greatest painters. Born in Urbino, he studied in Florence before being called to Rome to decorate the state rooms in the Vatican Palace. He painted for popes as well as for private patrons before his death at age 37 in 1520.

The interior of La Scala, Milan's prestigious opera house, was painted by an unknown artist in 1830. Built in 1778, the building hosted first productions of important operas by Verdi, Puccini, and other great composers. Opera has its roots in the singing, dancing, and poetry shows that entertained members of the Italian court in the early seventeenth century. The composer Jacopo Peri is considered to have composed the first opera.

New York's Little Italy was home to many newly arrived Italian immigrants in the early twentieth century. Today, it is still a vibrant community proud of its ethnic heritage. Above, a greengrocer in Little Italy surveys the street scene.

The streets of Little Italy celebrate the residents' dual heritage with Italian and American flags.

The Festival of San Gennaro, New York's largest street fair, is an opportunity for Little Italy's merchants to showcase their foods and products. The event has been a tradition since the mid-1920s. During the festival, the saint's statue is traditionally covered with offerings of flowers and money.

Colored lights decorate the streets of Little Italy during one of the neighborhood's traditional street fairs.

Boston's North End is home to a thriving Italian American community. Above, Italian American youths participate in the Fishermen's Festival, one of many Italian street fairs celebrated throughout the summer.

An elderly Italian American resident of Boston's North End has witnessed the gradual change in mainstream American attitudes toward Italian Americans. Your own elders will no doubt have interesting observations about being Italian American in earlier decades.

Al Pacino, a New York City native and Academy Award-winning Italian American actor, has powerfully portrayed some of cinema's best-known Italian American characters, such as Michael Corleone in the *Godfather* trilogy and Frank Serpico in *Serpico*.

Geraldine Ferraro gives the thumbs-up sign to her fellow Democrats at the Democratic National Convention in 1984, the year that Ferraro became the first woman vice-presidential candidate of a major U.S. political party. Ferraro and Walter Mondale ran against Ronald Reagan and George Bush. Before the election, Ferraro was a member of the U.S. House of Representatives for two terms.

For any organizational system you'll need a few basic supplies:

- File cabinets, crates, or boxes. These containers will hold all your artifacts, documentation, and other notes.
- File folders. Since many of the artifacts will be papers—birth and death certificates, immigration records, and so on, you will find it helpful to keep all information about each family group in a separate folder.
- Notebooks. You will need at least two notebooks. One (spiral or looseleaf) will be used for your note-taking during interviews or at the library, historical society, or other archive. The other notebook (looseleaf, with dividers) will contain all the documentation you'll need to create your family history book. It will contain everything you gather during your research—letters, photographs, clippings, wills, certificates of birth, marriage, and death, and so on. It will also contain the family group sheets and pedigree charts described below. It may also contain sections for oral history, correspondence, and other materials.

  Your notebook will soon become an indispensable resource for you and anyone else from whom you seek additional information. Because your notebooks contain so much important information, be sure that your name, address, and phone number are in each one.

  Even if you are doing most of your work on a computer, you will still need notebooks for your interview and library notes, and for holding the family sheets and other documents you will eventually print from your computer files.

- Forms: Family group sheets and pedigree charts. These sheets and charts are the forms you will use to record the fruits of your research—the names and vital statistics of your ancestors. Examples of typical forms and a detailed discussion of their purpose and use follow later in this chapter. You can make your own forms based on those in this book, or buy preprinted ones from a bookstore or genealogical supply house. If you are using a computer, you will find a number of software packages that generate these forms.

The family group sheets are worksheets on which you record information about family groups. Although these sheets are generally set up to record information about a traditional family, they are flexible and can be adapted to record various nontraditional family arrangements.

The pedigree chart is a sort of "road map" that shows family lines at a glance. The pedigree chart will contain information about each generation of the family you are researching. When it is completed, you will be able to start with one person (usually you) and trace the generations back as far as you have had time to research.

- Computer help. You do not need a computer to research your family history, but computers have become a great help to genealogists. Census data, vital records indexes, and other sources of information are increasingly available on CD-ROM. Many software packages are now available to help you in almost every phase of your research, from searching for relatives to writing up your family history. (See the **Resources** at the end of this chapter for some of the genealogical software now available.)

The Church of Jesus Christ of Latter-day Saints was one of the first organizations to provide such software. Their Personal Ancestral File (PAF) is a storage system for the data you collect about your family. You enter data, and the program puts it in place and lets you print it out in any number of ways.

Most software will print out family group sheets, pedigree charts, and family trees. Some will even print out these forms with images of your ancestors from old photographs that you scanned into the computer.

If organization is not one of your strong points, you may want to look into buying a commercial software package to do this part of the task for you.

- Photo album. Old photographs will turn out to be among the most interesting and useful artifacts of your search. Get photo albums with protective coverings on each page to protect old, curled, or cracking photos.
- Tape recorder or video camera. These are optional. You may find that they are especially useful if you are doing detailed oral histories. (See Chapter 4.)

Rules of Genealogical Research

There are three general rules in genealogical research:

- Start with what you know and branch out from there.
- Note the source of every piece of information, whether it is a name you unearthed in the 1910 census, or a photo provided by your Aunt Maria.
- Obtain proof of all facts with an official primary source document such as a birth certificate, marriage license, last will and testament, or naturalization certificate. You will learn more about primary sources and how to find them in Chapter 5.

If you keep these general rules in mind as you carry out your research, you family tree will grow more quickly and your information will be more accurate.

Starting with the first rule, begin your research with what you know best—yourself! To begin, simply turn to a page of your notebook and write down every fact you know about yourself: your full name, birthdate, birthplace, where you live now, who your relatives are, and so on. Now you need documentation for what you just wrote. That might seem unnecessary at first, but documentation is the bedrock of genealogical research, the foundation upon which you construct your family history. One weak brick, one incorrect name or date, could make the whole structure fragile and unreliable.

Although you probably know your own birthdate and birthplace, there is always a chance that you don't. Perhaps you think you were born in Chattanooga because that is where you and your whole family have always lived. How surprised you would be to learn that you were actually born in St. Louis and taken to Chattanooga when you were three days old. The only way to know something for sure is to have documentation—in this case, a birth certificate.

It is a good idea to start finding documentation and filing it from the very beginning. First get a copy of your birth certificate and file it in a folder with your name on it. Read your birth certificate and familiarize yourself with the kind of information it gives: date and place of birth, full name of the person born, and the names of the parents. Some birth certificates also include the parents' places of birth.

Branching Out

Now you are ready to branch out to other members of your family. Turn to another page in your notebook. Write the name of a relative at the top of the page and then write down every fact you know about that person. Following the general rule of starting with what you know, begin with the relative you know best. This may be a parent, a grandparent, an aunt, an uncle, or even a sibling. After you write down this information, search for documents to verify it. Again, a birth certificate is generally the best place to start.

After finding a birth certificate, you can begin gathering other information about yourself and your family from a number of sources, including the following:

- Newspaper clippings. Newspapers are a valuable source for genealogists, as they generally contain birth announcements, obituaries (death announcements), and announcements of engagement, marriage, military service, and so on.
- Church records. Church records have some of the same information found in newspaper clippings and can be used to verify that information. In church

A relative's passport application may provide useful information. Above, Italian American men wait in line for passports at the New York City Custom House in 1919.

records you may find documentation of a person's birth, baptism, confirmation or first communion, death, and burial.

- Family Bible. A family Bible may also contain birth, marriage, and death information.
- Family photographs. Old family photos will often bring to life the statistics you found in church records or newspaper clippings. If you are lucky, a relative will have made a notation on the back of the photograph. For example, "Antonio and Mary's wedding, 5/16/ 48." Such photos will become not only a source of documentation, but powerful remembrance of one of your ancestors.
- School records. Report cards, diplomas, and special awards will help you learn more about your ancestors and will also sometimes serve to verify names and dates.
- Employment records. Records showing where, when,

and by whom a person was employed will help you
flesh out that person's life.

- Court documents. Marriage and divorce papers,
  deeds, tax records, and other court actions are valuable sources of reliable information. Because they are
  legal documents, you can be almost one hundred
  percent sure that they are accurate.
- Military service and discharge papers. These are also a
  useful source of documentation since they too are
  legal documents.

As you find each document, write the source of your
information on the back of each photocopy or on a paper
clipped to the item. Then place it in the correct family
folder. Your notes should include when and where you saw
or copied the item, and where the item is now or who has it.
You may also write down any other interesting or useful
information.

The source of your information becomes very important if
later in your research you get conflicting information. For
example, suppose your grandmother gives you a picture and
says it is your Aunt Izzie when she was nineteen. You make
a note of this information and also note that it was your
grandmother who gave it to you. You file the information in
Aunt Izzie's file folder. Later, though, when you interview
your aunt, you show her the picture and she says that it is in
fact her younger sister. Now you'll have to weigh the evidence and decide who is right. In this case, you could fairly
conclude that your Aunt Izzie knows if the picture is of her
or not. Of course, it would be a good idea to ask other
people just to make sure.

Family Group Sheets

A family group sheet is exactly what its name implies. It is a
listing of the immediate family of one particular couple
(married or not), their children, their parents, and other
relatives. A typical group sheet has spaces for data on each
person and for the source of the data.

Start by filling out a family group sheet for your own family, and then work backward in time, generation by generation. You will begin filling in family group sheets as soon as you begin looking up people's dates of birth, marriage, death, and so on. Always use a pencil on genealogical forms until you are sure your data are absolutely correct. Then use a black ballpoint pen, as this will photocopy most clearly. You will begin making photocopies of the sheets as you write to relatives, requesting their help in providing information that will help you complete certain family groups.

Look at the sample family group sheet. Sheets like this are available from a number of sources, which are listed at the end of this chapter. Although you can make your own family group sheets, it is best to use preprinted ones. Then you can be sure that you are recording all relevant information. Using standardized sheets also allows you to share your research more easily with other genealogists.

Here are a few things to remember as you fill in the family group sheets:

- Always use full names and always use the maiden name of married women who have taken their husband's name.
- Record the father's name at the top of the family group sheet.
- If a man or woman has been married more than once, make a separate family group sheet for each marriage.
- If you are recording information for a large family, you may need more than one page. Be sure to number the pages.
- As you record each piece of data, write the source of the information and any additional information, such as the person's occupation, or years spent in military service. The source becomes important when you have conflicting data and have to decide which source is more reliable.
- Keep each family group sheet and all additional information and data in a family folder.

FAMILY GROUP WORK SHEET #_____

HUSBAND, Name:		WIFE, Name:	
Birth:	Place:	Birth:	Place:
Death:	Place:	Death:	Place:
Burial:	Place:	Burial:	Place:
Father:		Father:	
Mother:		Mother:	
Occupation:		Occupation:	
Notes:		Notes:	

Name	Date & Place of Birth	Date & Place of Marriage	Date & Place of Death	Married to	Date & Place of Birth Death

- Fill out the group sheets as completely as you can, tracking down all birthdates and birthplaces, parents' and grandparents' names, places and dates of marriage, names of children, and so on.
- Keep a list of the information you still need to discover concerning a particular family group. Clip this list to the family group sheet. Cross off items as you find the information.

Pedigree Charts

You may think pedigree is a word referring only to purebred dogs or horses, but it is also a genealogical term. It means a record of the generations of a family. Look at the sample pedigree chart. It shows at a glance the generations of a family and vital statistics, date and place of birth, marriage, and death. Put your name in the middle of the left-hand side of the page. Your father's name goes above and a bit to the right, and your mother's name below and to the right. This pattern continues, with males on the top line of a pair, and females on the bottom line. While this may annoy some female genealogists, it is the standard convention.

As with the family group sheets, it is best to use preprinted pedigree charts. You can find charts that cover from three to nine generations. When a family line is filled in all the way to the right margin, that family line is continued on another pedigree chart. The pedigree chart is designed to be flexible—by adding more pages, the chart can go back as far as you are willing to go.

To begin your own pedigree chart, fill in your name and vital statistics on the lines on the middle of the left-hand side of the chart. Then fill in the information for as many generations as you are sure of. Your paternal (father's) side of the family will be on the top half of the chart, and your maternal (mother's) side of the family will be on the lower half. As you proceed in your research, you will gradually fill in the pedigree chart. Include as much information as you can at each step of your research. Information will fall into four basic categories: names, dates, places, and relationships.

The accepted style for filling out a pedigree chart is to list each person by last name, then first name, then middle name. The last name is generally written in capital letters. Underneath each name are the person's date and place of birth, marriage, and death. The accepted style for recording dates is day, then month, then year. For example, your mother's birthdate may be written 1 October 1955. For places, start with the most specific location and move to the broader one. For example, "Ellis Street, Chicago, Cook

Pedigree Chart

Name of Compiler _____

Address _____

City, State _____

Date _____

Person No.1 on this chart is the same person as No._____ on chart No._____.

Chart No._____

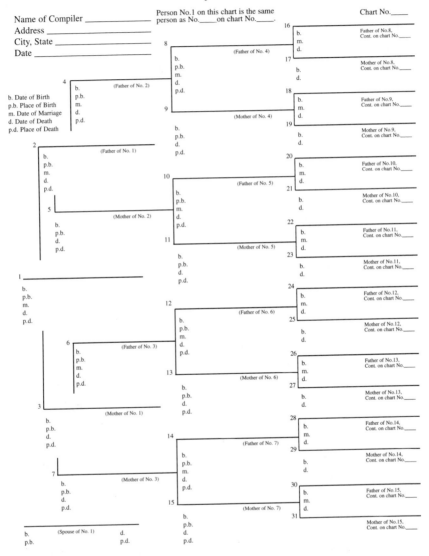

b. Date of Birth
p.b. Place of Birth
m. Date of Marriage
d. Date of Death
p.d. Place of Death

16
b.
m.
d.
Father of No.8,
Cont. on chart No._____

17
b.
d.
Mother of No.8,
Cont. on chart No._____

18
b.
m.
d.
Father of No.9,
Cont. on chart No._____

19
b.
d.
Mother of No.9,
Cont. on chart No._____

20
b.
m.
d.
Father of No.10,
Cont. on chart No._____

21
b.
d.
Mother of No.10,
Cont. on chart No._____

22
b.
m.
d.
Father of No.11,
Cont. on chart No._____

23
b.
d.
Mother of No.11,
Cont. on chart No._____

24
b.
m.
d.
Father of No.12,
Cont. on chart No._____

25
b.
d.
Mother of No.12,
Cont. on chart No._____

26
b.
m.
d.
Father of No.13,
Cont. on chart No._____

27
b.
d.
Mother of No.13,
Cont. on chart No._____

28
b.
m.
d.
Father of No.14,
Cont. on chart No._____

29
b.
d.
Mother of No.14,
Cont. on chart No._____

30
b.
m.
d.
Father of No.15,
Cont. on chart No._____

31
b.
d.
Mother of No.15,
Cont. on chart No._____

8
(Father of No. 4)
b.
p.b.
m.
d.
p.d.

9
(Mother of No. 4)
b.
p.b.
d.
p.d.

10
(Father of No. 5)
b.
p.b.
m.
d.
p.d.

11
(Mother of No. 5)
b.
p.b.
d.
p.d.

12
(Father of No. 6)
b.
p.b.
m.
d.
p.d.

13
(Mother of No. 6)
b.
p.b.
d.
p.d.

14
(Father of No. 7)
b.
p.b.
m.
d.
p.d.

15
(Mother of No. 7)
b.
p.b.
d.
p.d.

4
(Father of No. 2)
b.
p.b.
m.
d.
p.d.

5
(Mother of No. 2)
b.
p.b.
d.
p.d.

6
(Father of No. 3)
b.
p.b.
m.
d.
p.d.

7
(Mother of No. 3)
b.
p.b.
d.
p.d.

2
(Father of No. 1)
b.
p.b.
m.
d.
p.d.

3
(Mother of No. 1)
b.
p.b.
d.
p.d.

1 _____
b.
p.b.
m.
d.
p.d.

(Spouse of No. 1)
b.
p.b.
d.
p.d.

County, Illinois." These ways of recording information will make it easier for you to identify and look up missing information when you are in a library or archive. The other reason to follow accepted standards is to make it easier to request further information from relatives, libraries, archives, and other sources of genealogical information.

You may want to take copies of your pedigree charts to libraries and archives and on interviews. They will help guide you as you get involved in the details of your research.

File Keeping

Each person has his or her own way of organizing files, but here are some suggestions that may help you:

- Make a file folder for each family group.
- Record the last name first on the file label.
- File each piece of documentation in the folder for the family to whom it relates.
- File individual folders in your file cabinet or box in alphabetical order by last name, then first name.
- Create a table of contents for each folder that lists the documents in the folder.

Just as there are many ways to organize your files, there are many ways to pursue your genealogy. They range from library research to interviews with your relatives to sleuthing in family photo albums, scrapbooks, and letters. You may choose nearly any starting point and branch out from there. If one avenue leads to a temporary dead end, there are always other avenues to pursue. Often you will find that as you go down another road in search of other information, you will come across the information that you needed when you ran into the earlier dead end.

The following chapters will tell you how to go about tracking down the information you need to fill out your family group sheets and pedigree charts.

Resources

ORGANIZING YOUR RESEARCH

American Genealogy: A Basic Course. Arlington: National Genealogical Society.

> A home-study program available from the NGS, 4527 17th Street North, Arlington, VA 22207-2363. It includes written and video material. It is a great preview of the organizational and research skills necessary to facilitate your research.

Clark, Donna K. *The Ancestor Detective*. **Arvada, CO: Ancestor Publishers, 1976.**

> A workbook to help you research, file, and retrieve information about your ancestors.

Dollarhide, William. *Managing a Genealogical Project: A Complete Manual for the Management and Organization of Genealogical Materials*. **Baltimore: Genealogical Publishing Co., 1988.**

> Many tips on how to organize your genealogical search. A great book to read before beginning your research.

Eakle, Arlene, and Cerny, Johni, eds. *The Source: A Guidebook of American Genealogy*. **Salt Lake City, UT: Ancestry Incorporated, 1984.**

> This lengthy volume will serve as a useful reference at various points in your research. It includes sections on major record sources, published genealogical sources, special sources, and appendixes. Also provides locations and phone numbers for state and regional archives and historical and genealogical societies.

Everton, George B. *A Handy Book for Genealogists.* **Logan, UT: Everton Publishers, 1989.**

> Everton is one of the largest publishers of genealogical books and magazines. This is a good guide for the beginner.

Jaussi, Laureen Richards, and Chaston, Gloria Duncan. *Fundamentals of Genealogical Reasearch.* **Salt Lake City, UT: Deseret Book Co., 1972.**

> A good overview of the research process.

Nichols, Elizabeth L. "The International Genealogical Index." *New England Historical and Genealogical Register,* **Vol. 137, July, 1983, pp. 193–217.**

> Explains what the IGI is and how to use it. The IGI contains many birth, christening, and marriage entries.

Williams, Dorthy Lazelle. *Genealogy Vocabulary Aids.* **Sacramento: D. L. Williams, 1985.**

> This helpful book contains a dictionary of genealogical terms, a list of common names and nicknames, abbreviations commonly used in genealogy, and other research aids.

GENERAL RULES AND PROCEDURES

Baxter, Angus. *Dos and Don'ts for Ancestor Hunters.* **Baltimore: Genealogical Publishing Co., 1988.**

> A good book to read at the beginning of your research.

Calberg, Nancy Ellen. *Overcoming Dead Ends.* **Anaheim, CA: Carlberg Press, 1991.**

> An important book to turn to when you get stuck in your research.

Chase, Scott B. *Why Are There No Tall Grandmas?* **New York: Interlaken, 1990.**

A guide to assist you in researching your family history.

Drake, Paul E. *In Search of Family History: A Starting Place.* **Bowie, MD: Heritage Books, 1992.**

A good book for the beginner who might be overwhelmed by the task of genealogical research.

Eicholz, Alice. *Discovering Your Heritage: An Introduction to Family History.* **Salt Lake City, UT: Ancestry Incorporated, 1987.**

The basics of genealogical research.

Family History. A fifty-one-episode made-for-cable TV show that emphasizes the fun of genealogical research. Each episode focuses on a particular aspect of genealogy, including particular heritage searches. The program also focuses on practical matters like using archives and censuses and computer software. It can be obtained on videotape from: Stephen Conte, P.O. Box 962, West Caldwell, NJ 07007.

Gray, Nancy. *Compiling Your Family History.* **Sydney: Australian Society of Genealogists, 1979.**

A manual for documenting family histories and genealogical records.

Greenwood, Val D. *The Researcher's Guide to American Genealogy.* **Baltimore: Genealogical Publishing Co., 1990.**

An excellent book to start with. It leads you to an intermediate level of research and then points you toward more advanced resources.

Heimberg, Marilyn Markham. *Discover Your Roots.* **San Diego: Communication Creativity, 1977.**

An easy guide for tracing your family tree.

Hilton, Suzanne. *Who Do You Think You Are? Digging for Your Family Roots.* **Philadelphia: Westminster Press, 1977.**

A good book to read before you begin your search. It is written specifically for young researchers, who may not have had much experience in libraries and archives.

Lackey, Richard S. *Cite Your Sources: A Manual for Documenting Family Histories and Genealogical Records.* **New Orleans: Polyanthos, 1980.**

The best book for valuable information on documentation. Properly documenting your sources will both help you in retracing your steps and ease the path of others who may want to continue your research.

Lichtman, Allan J. *Your Family History: How to Use Oral History, Personal Family Archives, and Public Documents to Discover Your Heritage.* **New York: Vintage, 1978.**

Read this book before beginning your research to decide in which areas you may want to concentrate your research.

Pehrson, Helga. *Order.* **Logan, UT: Everton Publishers, 1976.**

The title says it all. This book will help you organize and order your research.

Rubincam, Milton, ed. *Genealogical Research: Methods and Sources.* **Washington, DC: American Society of Genealogists, 1981.**

A good source of background information.

———. *Pitfalls in Genealogical Research.* **Salt Lake City, UT: Ancestry Incorporated, 1987.**

Another book to read before you start your research, so as to avoid pitfalls.

Westin, Jeane Eddy. *Finding Your Roots: How Every American Can Trace His Ancestors—at Home and Abroad.* **Los Angeles: J. P. Tarcher, 1977.**

A comprehensive guide to genealogical research, with sections on specific ethnic groups.

Wright, Norman E. *Preserving Your American Heritage.* **Provo, UT: Brigham Young University Press, 1981.**

Deals with the hows and whys of genealogical research and explains why such research is so engaging to so many people.

FAMILY GROUP SHEETS

Schreiner-Yantis Family Group Sheets.

Netti Schreiner-Yantis designed what is considered the best family group sheet, as well as pedigree charts and other forms. Write for a price list. GBIP, 6818 Lois Drive, Springfield, VA 22150.

Evelyn Spears Family Group Sheet Exchange
East 12502 Frideger Street
Elk, WA 99009

This service provides previously researched family group sheets for the requested surname. The charge is about ten dollars per surname, with a catalog of 14,000 surnames.

Genealogical Center, Inc.
International Family Group Sheet Exchange
P.O. Box 17698
Tampa, FL 33682

This service charges thirty cents per page, and each completed surname study is from ten to 300 pages long. Write for their catalog of 8,000 surnames.

COMPUTER GENEALOGY

Computers can be very useful to genealogists. Many genealogical software programs have been developed to assist with
tasks such as chart-making, journal-keeping, family tree
design, and record storage. The Internet also offers many
resources such as genealogical discussion groups and online
access to libraries and archives. For information on genealogical software programs, consult a local software dealer, or
refer to the quarterly magazine *Genealogical Computing*,
which publishes a yearly genealogical software directory.

Genealogical Computing

> Ancestry Incorporated
> 440 South 400 West, Building D
> Salt Lake City, UT 84101
> 800-531-1790

INTERNET RESOURCES

Everton Publishers Genealogy Page

> http://www.everton.com

Genealogy Home Page

> ftp ftp.cac.psu.edu/pub/genealogy
> http://ftp.cac.psu.edu/~saw/genealogy.html

Italian Genealogy Homepage

> http://www.xs4all.nl/\/tardio/index.html

Joe's Italian Genealogy Page

> http://www.phoenix.net/\/joe

LDS Research Guides

> ftp hipp.etsu.edu/pub/genealogy

U.S. Census Bureau

> ftp gateway.census.gov/pub/genealogy
> ftp://gateway.census.gov
> http://www.census.gov

National Archives

gopher gopher.nara.gov
gopher://gopher.nara.gov
http://www.nara.gov

World Wide Web Genealogy Demo Page

http://demo.genweb.org/gene/genedemo.html

Chapter 4
Getting the Inside Story

Many people think that genealogical research takes place in the dusty rooms of a library, historical society, or county courthouse. Your search for data on your ancestors may eventually take you to such places, but often the easiest and best way to begin is by interviewing your relatives.

Interviews are of two general types: informational and anecdotal. An informational interview will give you the data you need to fill in your family group sheets and pedigree charts. The questions you ask in an informational interview are "closed-ended." This means they have a specific answer. For example, if you ask your aunt, "How many brothers and sisters did you have?" and she answers, "Six," you have your answer and can move on to the next question.

Anecdotal interviews have quite a different objective. Their primary goal is not to get data, but to elicit detailed stories and memories. An anecdotal interview asks "open-ended" questions that have no right or wrong answer. They are broad and are designed to introduce a topic of discussion that will lead to a variety of stories and reminiscences. For example, you might ask an uncle, "How did you feel about growing up in such a big family?" to get him to tell you stories of his younger days and home life.

While informational interviews provide the raw material to fill in your family group sheets and pedigree charts, anecdotal interviews provide the raw material for oral histories and are often called oral history interviews. Oral histories are discussed later in this chapter.

Interviewing for Charts
To find the information you need to fill out your family

group sheets and pedigree charts, you can interview close relatives as well as old neighbors, godparents, teachers, and colleagues of your subjects. The first step in preparing for an interview is to create a questionnaire. You can use the questionnaire as a script in face-to-face interviews or send it to people you cannot meet in person.

The basic information you need for your pedigree charts includes:

- Full name
- Nicknames
- Birthdate and birthplace
- Wedding date and place (if applicable)
- Number and names of children (if applicable)
- Death date and place of burial (if applicable)

Information for the family group sheets might include:

- Jobs held by various family members
- Where family members went to school
- If and where they served in the military
- If and how they were involved in their communities
- Hobbies and interests
- Religious affiliations

Formulate questions that will elicit this sort of information. Many of the **Resources** at the end of the chapter provide sample questionnaires. Record answers to your questions in your note-taking notebook. You may choose to tape record the interview in addition to taking notes. If so, be sure to get the person's permission before you turn on the recorder. Even if the person is self-conscious about being recorded, you'll find that most people forget about the recorder once the interview is underway.

Additional areas to explore with your interviewee may include:

- Information in a family cemetery or at a grave site
- Accomplished or famous people in a branch of the family tree

- Any other family member who has traced part of the family history
- The existence of scrapbooks, old photos, letters, diaries, journals, the family Bible, etc.

Interviewing Dos and Don'ts

- Preparation. Before the interview, prepare thoroughly so as not to waste your and your interviewee's time. Be sure you know at least the bare facts about your interviewee. Review these facts as you begin the interview and ask for corrections before moving on into unknown territory.
- Specific, concise questions. Remember the "five W's" that journalists use to formulate their questions and get the facts: Who, what, where, when, why (and sometimes how). Speak clearly and get to the point.
- Be a good listener. Remember that you are there to gather information, not to talk about yourself or your project.
- Length. You do not want to tire or annoy the interviewee. Interviews should be short—under one hour. If you feel more time is needed, arrange for a follow-up interview on another day.
- People present. Interviews should always be done in private. Your shy great-aunt may be less forthcoming if her garrulous husband is present.
- Corrections and additions. After the interview, review your notes or transcribe your tape. Type up the relevant information you gleaned from the interview and send a copy to the interviewee for corrections. This is a very valuable step in your research. Often you'll find that your interview started the person thinking. When he or she gets the written copy, additional names, dates, or places may come to mind. Encourage the person to correct or add information to what you have typed.
- Thank you. When you send the notes to the interviewee, be sure to thank him or her for their time and

Interviewing elderly relatives offers a way to preserve precious memories as well as to gather important genealogical information. Even if your relatives do not remember life in Italy, they may have heard stories passed down from their elders. Above, the author's great-grandmother poses for a formal portrait.

the valuable information provided. Also offer to send the person a copy of the completed family history if he or she wants one.

Mail Interviews

If your interview subjects live far from you, it will be easier to contact them by mail. To do this, first write a cover letter explaining who you are, what you are doing, and why you are writing. The letter should also thank the person in advance for helping.

Along with the cover letter, send your interview questionnaire form. You may also enclose copies of partially completed pedigree charts and family group sheets so the person knows what information you have.

The cover letter is a very important document. A polite, honest, well-written letter will improve the chances that a person will help you. A rude or badly written letter will probably go with the day's junk mail. You can model your letter on the one below or ones in a source at the end of this chapter.

Dear _____:

I am _____, the son/daughter/other relative of _____. I am writing to ask if you could help me gather information about the ____ family. I would be grateful if you could find the time to answer the enclosed questionnaire and add to the information on the enclosed pedigree chart. If you find any mistakes on the chart, please let me know. When you have finished, please return the questionnaire and chart in the stamped, self-addressed envelope that I have enclosed.

It would be a great help if you could also tell me who else in the ____ family might have information about ____ or if you have any information or documents that I might copy and return. I want to record and preserve the ____ family's history as accurately and completely as possible.

When I have completed my research I would be happy to send you a copy of the results. Please let me know if you would like to receive a copy of my completed family history.

Thank you very much for your time and help.

Sincerely,
[your signature]

Old Photos

Old photographs are some of the most evocative and precious links with your family's past. There is nothing like a picture of your great-grandmother to tell you something of her personality and the hardships of her life in the "old country." Old photos can also tell you what your relatives looked like when they were young, what their homes and towns were like, and other important biographical and geographical facts.

How a picture was taken, who took it, and who is in the picture can tell you many important facts that will help advance your research. You may be able to date a person's marriage or determine their place of birth or number of children from the information in a photo or written on the back of it.

If you are lucky, you may find all the information you need written on the back of the photos. For example a picture of a small boy might say *Giuseppe Castiglia, 6 meses*. And the back of the photo might show a photographer's stamp giving the date and location of the studio that developed the photo. From these bits of information you can get a good idea of the date and place of birth of your ancestor Giuseppe. Often school photos include a signboard with the name of the school and the year. This also can tell you more about a particular person.

Unfortunately, many photos have no notations on them, and you may have to deduce information from the picture. A landmark such as the Statue of Liberty or the Sears Tower can tell where a photo was taken; the model of the cars and the style of clothing can tell you when. Photographers' stamps on the back can also place and date the photo.

If you have a camera, you can use it to photograph old photos, Bible records, tombstones, living relatives, family reunions, heirlooms, and historic structures. Such pictures will bring life to your final family history.

Oral History Interviews

The oral history interview is different from the informational interview. Although you may begin with the journalist's five W's (who, what, where, when, why), you will end up with more "Why" and "How" questions that allow the person to speak freely about his or her life. You might first ask, "When did your family move to Tennessee?" But as soon as you know the answer, you will ask, "How did you feel about moving to Tennessee?"

You can hold oral history interviews with the people you contacted for informational interviews, as well as other family members, friends, neighbors, colleagues, teachers, and so on. The first step is to decide whom you want to interview. Then contact the person to request the interview, mentioning why you have asked to speak with him or her. If the person agrees, make an appointment, keeping the interview under two hours long. If the interview goes well and you feel the person has more to say, you can always arrange another session.

When you make the appointment, mention that you will ask the person to sign a release upon completion of the interview. Assure the person that you will respect his or her privacy and will keep any or all information confidential if he or she wishes. If you want to audiotape or videotape the interview, ask permission first.

Conduct the interview in a quiet, private place where you will not be interrupted. While note-taking works well for the short answers a person gives in an informational interview, you'll find that audiotape or videotape is a better way of recording the stories told in an oral history interview. If you use a tape recorder, it is best to use a small, unobtrusive one. If you are videotaping the interview, set the camera on a tripod so that it does not distract the interviewee. Whether audio or video, use a tape that runs 120 minutes so that you will not have to break the flow of the interview by fiddling with machines. (Many books with helpful hints about audiotaping and videotaping oral history interviews are listed in the **Resources**.)

After you have set up your recording equipment, take a few minutes to talk casually with the person. When you both feel at ease, you are ready to begin the interview. First, "label" your tape with a sentence such as, "This is [interviewee's] oral history interview with [your name], at [location] on [month, day, year]." It's a good idea to play this introduction back to make sure your equipment is working before going on with the interview.

Have a list of "open-ended" questions handy, but do not feel that you must ask all of them. An oral history interview should have a rather loose format. Don't be afraid to let the interviewee's interests and memories take over the session. If the interview goes well, you'll be able to ignore your own questions and just ask follow-up questions.

The most important rule is to be a good listener. A good listener maintains eye contact and encourages the speaker with phrases like "I see" and "Really?" Never interrupt. If you want to ask follow-up questions, wait until the person pauses after finishing a story or thought.

You should also "listen" to the person's body language. Notice facial expressions and gestures. These can give clues to the feelings behind the words. For example, if the person finishes a story by saying, "Yeah, I guess you could say I've had a hard life," a reader of the transcript may not know exactly what is meant unless you make a note of the body language. A shrug and downcast eyes would lend the sentence a very different meaning than a twinkle in the eye and a smile on the lips. If you transcribe an interview, body language such as smiles, shrugs, and hand gestures should appear in brackets.

The topics of an oral history interview can largely be left up to the interviewee. You should try, however, to ask questions specific to the person's experience. For instance, you might ask a person who came to this country at the age of eighteen to talk about life in Italy before he or she emigrated, or his or her first impressions of America. If the person was born to immigrant parents, you might ask how Italian traditions were maintained in the home.

Coax the interviewee's memories about specific people, places, and events. If you want or need to ask sensitive, personal questions about death, money, divorce, or health, wait until you have achieved a comfortable rapport with the interviewee. Then reassure the person that it is not necessary to answer and that you will keep the responses confidential if he or she wishes.

At the end of the interview, thank the person and ask him or her to sign an interview release. The form might look like this:

> I [interviewee's name] consent to have my interview with [your name] recorded on [audio/video] tape, and I voluntarily grant permission to [your name] for full use of the interview for the purpose of compiling a family history. I understand that I may have a typed copy of the interview upon request. [Interviewee's signature]   [Date]

Remember that this signed release does not give you the right to use the interview to embarrass or cause pain to anyone.

After each interview, file your notes, transcripts, and any documents you have photocopied or photographs you have taken in the appropriate file folder.

After each interviewee has verified the information you gleaned from an interview, fill in any new or different information on your family group sheets and pedigree charts. Remember to record the source for each piece of data.

Organization is particularly important for photos. Be very careful with old photos, which are often fragile. File them in your photo albums for easy identification. Keep a record of each photo and what you know about it, including the subject(s), where it was taken, when, and by whom. You should also note who gave or lent you the photo and what information about it you have corroborated with another source.

Each time you write a letter, file a copy of it in the appropriate folder. As you receive answers, attach them to the original letter.

Resources

INTERVIEWING

Alessi, Jean, and Miller, Jan. *Once Upon a Memory: Your Family Tales and Treasures*. **White Hall, VA: Betterway Publications, 1987.**

How to elicit your family members' stories and record them for future generations.

Banaka, William H. *Training in Depth Interviewing*. **New York: Harper and Row, 1971.**

This book contains tips for preparing for interviews, staying on track, and eliciting good answers. It will help you become a skilled and productive interviewer.

McLaughlin, Eve. *Interviewing Elderly Relatives*. **Plymouth, U.K.: Federation of Family History Societies, 1985.**

Contains many useful tips for interviewing older relatives.

Price, Bob. *Family Memories: A Guide to Reminiscing*. **New South Wales, Australia: State Library of New South Wales, 1992.**

Another useful "how-to" book for family history interviews.

Stano, Michael E., and Reinsch, N. L., Jr. *Communication in Interviews*. **Englewood Cliffs, NJ: Prentice-Hall, 1982.**

Advice on interviewing techniques, preparation, communicating your questions clearly, and reading verbal and nonverbal signals from your interviewee.

OLD PHOTOS

Eakle, Arlene H. *Photograph Analysis*. **Salt Lake City, UT: Family History World, 1976.**

A useful book for techniques to discover the date and place of a photo.

Earnest, Russell D. *Grandma's Attic: Making Heirlooms Part of Your Family History*. **Albuquerque, NM: R. D. Earnest Assoc., 1991.**

This book details the significance of china, quilts, silver, furniture, and other objects owned by your ancestors.

Frisch-Ripley, Karen. *Unlocking the Secret in Old Photographs*. **Salt Lake City, UT: Ancestry, Incorporated, 1991.**

This book gives many helpful hints and techniques for dating and analyzing your old family photos.

Frost, Lenore. *Dating Family Photos, 1850–1920*. **Essedon, Victoria, Australia: L. Frost, 1991.**

This book is written by an Australian, but her tips on dating photos are also useful for American researchers.

ORAL HISTORY

Allen, Barbara, and Montell, William Lynwood. *From Memory to History: Using Oral Sources in Local Historical Research*. **Nashville, TN: American Association for State and Local History, 1981.**

Many helpful hints on how to use oral histories.

Baum, Willa K. *Transcribing and Editing Oral History*. **Nashville: American Association of State and Local History, 1981.**

Although this book tells you what to do after you have conducted an oral history interview, it would be a good idea to read it before conducting the interview so that you can ask the right questions and guide your interviewee toward reminiscences that will need less editing.

Brown, Cynthia Stokes. *Like It Was: A Complete Guide to Writing Oral History*. **New York: Teachers and Writers Collaborative, 1988.**

This user-friendly guide gives the nitty-gritty of writing up your oral histories. It provides instructions for writing oral histories and biographies, including planning, interviewing, transcribing, editing, and publishing the results.

Cohen, David Steven, ed. *America, the Dream of My Life*. **New Brunswick: Rutgers University Press, 1990.**

This collection contains selections from the Federal Writers' Project New Jersey Ethnic Survey. It includes many oral history excerpts from Italian Americans, detailing their social life, customs, and biographies.

Davis, Cullom; Back, Kathryn; and MacLean, Kay. *Oral History: From Tape to Type*. **Chicago: American Library Association, 1977.**

This book helps you take all those tapes and convert them into part of your family history.

Epstein, Ellen Robinson, and Mendelsohn, Rona. *Record and Remember: Tracing Your Roots through Oral History*. **New York: Sovereign Books, 1978.**

A "how-to" book on using oral history as part of your genealogical research.

Fletcher, William P. *Talking Your Roots: Recording Your Family History*. **New York: Dodd, Mead, 1986.**

A guide to preserving oral history with videotape and audiotape. Provides suggested topics, questions, and interview techniques.

Gluck, Sherna Berger, and Patai, Daphne, eds. *Women's Words: The Feminist Practice of Oral History*. **New York: Routledge, 1991.**

Since women's lives have generally been part of oral, rather than written, history, this book comments on oral history from a feminist perspective.

Grele, Ronald J. *Envelope of Sound: The Art of Oral History*. **Chicago: Precedent Publishers, 1985.**

Includes interviews with some famous recorders of oral history such as Studs Terkel.

Hutching, Megan. *Talking History: A Short Guide to Oral History*. **Wellington, NZ: Bridget Williams Books, 1993.**

A concise and useful introduction to oral history.

Hoopes, James. *Oral History: An Introduction for Students*. **Chapel Hill: University of North Carolina Press, 1979.**

A useful first book for learning about oral history.

How to Interview Your Ancestors. **Baltimore: Genealogical Institute, 1974.**

This book contains many useful hints and techniques for getting the most from your interviews.

Jenkins, Sara, ed. *Past, Present: Recording Life Stories of Older People*. **Washington, DC: St. Albans Parish, 1978.**

You can order this "how-to" manual from the publications department of the National Council on Aging, 409 Third Street, SW, Washington, DC 20024.

LaGumina, Salvatore. *The Immigrants Speak: The Italian-Americans Tell Their Story*. **New York: Center for Migration Studies, 1978.**

Biography and oral history from generations of Italian Americans whose personal histories mirror their psychology and personalities.

Lanman, Barry Allen, and Mehaffy, George. *Oral History in the Secondary School Classroom.* **Provo, UT: Oral History Association, 1988.**

This book has many helpful hints that will apply to your genealogical research.

McLaughlin, Paul. *A Family Remembers: How to Create a Family Memoir Using Video and Tape Recorders.* **Bellingham, WA: Self-Counsel Press, 1993.**

If you want to use video or audio tape, be sure to read this book before you begin.

McMahan, Eva, and Rogers, Kim Lacy. *Interactive Oral History Interviewing.* **Hillsdale, NJ: Erlbaum Associates, 1994.**

This "how-to" book also gives hints on how to deal with the interviewee's subjectivity.

Pellegrini, Angelo. *Immigrant's Return.* **New York: Macmillan, 1952.**

The second volume of Pellegrini's autobiography traces his visit back to Italy.

Portelli, Alessandro. *The Death of Luigi Trastulli and Other Stories: Form and Meaning in Oral History.* **Albany, NY: SUNY Press, 1991.**

An example of the use of oral history to explore the lives of laborers in Terni, Italy, and in Harlan Country, Kentucky.

Santoli, Al. *The New Americans: An Oral History.* **New York: Viking, 1988.**

Immigrants and refugees who have come to the United States in recent decades.

Seifer, Nancy. *Nobody Speaks for Me: Self-Portraits of American Working Class Women.* **New York: Simon & Schuster, 1976.**

Oral histories of working-class women, including Italian Americans.

Shumway, Gary L., and Hartley, William G. *An Oral History Primer.* **Salt Lake City, UT: Primer Publications, 1981.**

An easy-to-use handbook for collecting oral histories.

Sitton, Than. *Oral History: A Guide for Teachers and Others.* **Austin: University of Texas Press, 1983.**

This guide is just as useful for students as for teachers.

Vitiello, Justin. *Poetics and Literature of the Sicilian Diaspora: Studies in Oral History and Story-Telling.* **San Francisco: Mellen Research University Press, 1993.**

This book focuses on Sicilian emigration and immigration in the twentieth century. It includes many interviews from those who left Sicily and those who were left behind.

Yow, Valerie R. *Recording Oral History: A Practical Guide.* **Thousand Oaks, CA: Sage Publications, 1994.**

This book outlines the methodology used by social scientists and other serious researchers who use oral history.

Chapter 5
Using Outside Sources

Primary and Secondary Sources

After obtaining verbal or written information from relatives
and others close to your family, you are ready to start documenting. Documentation can come from various sources
that fall into one of two categories: primary and secondary
sources.

Primary sources are those created at or around the time
an event occurred, usually by someone who had personal
knowledge of the event. They include official documents
such as birth certificates, school and church records, marriage licenses, immigration and naturalization records, and
driver's licenses, as well as unofficial documents such as
diaries, journals, letters, birth, wedding, and death announcements, old report cards, baptismal certificates, baby
books, awards, and greeting cards. A family Bible can be an
especially useful primary source, as family members may
have used it to record birth, marriage, and death dates.

Secondary sources are those created some time after an
event occurred. For example, a county courthouse may have
compiled a list of deaths some years or decades after those
deaths occurred. Secondary sources help point you toward
primary sources, which tend to be more reliable. They are
also crucial when no primary source exists. As your research
progresses back in time, fewer primary sources will be available. Many parts of the United States did not require the
recording of births, marriages, and deaths until the last part
of the nineteenth century. Similarly, the small, rural Italian
villages that your ancestors may have come from seldom
recorded these life events in any official manner. You then
have to rely on secondary sources such as indexes, local

histories, biographies, genealogies, and reference books. These sources are found in libraries, courthouses, and archives.

Primary sources can be found in public places, but more often they are found in private places. Attics, basements, and closets, for example, have been known to reveal treasures to genealogists. With the owner's permission, you might ask to look through these locations for artifacts such as baptismal and first communion certificates, ship manifests, and naturalization documents. Any records or documents you find should be photocopied and the originals returned to the owner as soon as possible.

Vital Records

Vital records are the official legal papers that record births, deaths, marriages, and divorces. They are one of the most useful types of primary sources. Not only do they give you accurate, reliable information, but they also further your research. Often a vital record takes you back to the previous generation by providing you with the names of the person's parents.

Vital records can be crucial in documenting your research and establishing its accuracy. For example, if your grandmother tells you that her mother was born in 1899, but your aunt remembers the date as 1897, one way to establish the fact is to find the birth certificate of your great-grandmother. If she has no birth certificate (this is often the case for relatives born in rural parts of Italy), another official paper such as a marriage license might help you verify the date.

Every state and country has a branch of government that maintains and dispenses information about vital records. In the United States, it is the Bureau of Vital Records or Department of Health. The offices are generally in the state capital. An excellent publication containing updated information is *Where to Write for Vital Records: Births, Deaths, Marriages, and Divorces.* You can request this leaflet from: Superintendent of Documents, U.S. Government Printing Office, Washington, DC 20402. Ask for document #017-

022-00847-5. Keep in mind that you may have to wait a month or more for a reply from a government office. Also, you must pay a small fee for a copy of vital records.

Visiting a Courthouse

You may also obtain copies of some vital records from county courthouses. Here are examples of the kinds of records kept at county courthouses and the facts you can learn from them.

Record	Information it contains
Marriage records	Woman's maiden name, marriage date, sometimes parents' names, ages and residences of the couple, where the marriage took place
Deed records	Purchases and sales of land and other property; the divisions of estates among heirs
Wills	How an estate is to be divided after someone's death; the names of the wife, children, and other relatives of the deceased
Civil and criminal lawsuits	Names of relatives (if they were ever involved in a lawsuit)

Before going to a courthouse, verify that the person you are researching lived in that county when he or she married, bought or sold land, etc. A few other pointers to keep in mind when you go to a courthouse in search of information are the following:

- Know what you want to know before you go.
- Speak briefly about your research objectives to someone on the staff; be courteous.
- Photocopies will probably be expensive. You may prefer to copy information instead.

When you have finished your research, whether it was successful or not, be sure to thank everyone who made records available to you.

Libraries and Archives

At some point in your research, you'll need to go to a library or archive in search of information. An archive is very much like a library. It is a place where public records or historical documents are kept. It may be found in a courthouse or church or in the private library of a person or organization.

Libraries and archives have many volumes containing both primary and secondary source material. This material includes published family histories, compilations of census records, local history publications, old newspapers, and manuscript collections of unpublished material such as diaries, journals, collections of letters, church records, and store ledgers.

If you are not familiar with the library or archive, ask the librarian for a quick tour. Explain that you are involved in genealogical research and will need to look at books, newspapers, and other documents to find information about your family history. Most larger libraries have a collection of local history and genealogical materials. The reference works by Marion J. Kaminkow (see **Resources**) list genealogies and local histories held by the Library of Congress in Washington, DC. If your library does not have the materials you need, ask a librarian about interlibrary loan, a service that is usually free for library patrons.

When your research leads you to the hometown of an ancestor that is not near your own town, you can write to the head librarian of libraries in that town and request information. Be polite in your letter and be specific about what you are looking for. You may model your letter on this one. (Find out the person's name by calling the library before you write.)

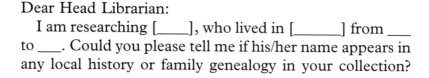

Dear Head Librarian:

I am researching [____], who lived in [_____] from ___ to ___. Could you please tell me if his/her name appears in any local history or family genealogy in your collection?

Also, could you direct me to any local genealogical, historical, or Italian American ethnic organizations that I might consult for my research?

Thank you very much for your time and help.

Sincerely,

———

Be sure to include a self-addressed, stamped envelope for a reply. The library may also charge a small fee for its services, including photocopying.

Your library will probably have old copies of the local newspaper stored on microfilm. They may carry other papers from the county or region as well. Old newspapers are a valuable source of information such as dates and places of births, weddings, and deaths. Obituaries often contain short biographies of the deceased. Additional biographical information can often be found in wedding and engagement announcements, career milestone announcements (a promotion or job change), and graduation announcements.

In looking for such announcements, a name index is helpful. If a newspaper has an index of names, you can simply look under your ancestors' names. Unfortunately, not all newspapers have name indexes. If yours does not, you will have to know the approximate date of the birth, marriage, death, or other event you are trying to track down and skim through those issues of the paper for the announcement in question.

In cities with large Italian American populations (New York, Boston, Philadelphia, Chicago), you may find old newspapers published exclusively by and for the Italian community. These newspapers covered the life events of local Italian Americans and their businesses and are therefore more likely to contain articles about your ancestors than the English-language press. They are good places to search for information about the family's first generation in

America. Since most of these papers are written in Italian, you may need a translator (perhaps an older relative) to help you read the relevant articles.

Most Italian-language newspapers are no longer published. Unfortunately, there is no single catalog or listing of them. You may find some newspapers available on microfilm. *Newspapers in Microform: United States 1948–1983* (2 vols.) (Washington D.C.: Library of Congress, 1984) lists many nineteenth- and early twentieth-century Italian-language newspapers that were microfilmed and reported to the Library of Congress by libraries across the country between 1948 and 1983. For a list of Italian-language newspapers still in print today, see Lubomyr R. and Anna T. Wynar's *Encyclopedic Directory of Ethnic Newspapers and Periodicals in the United States*, 2d ed. (Littleton, CO: Libraries Unlimited, Inc., 1976).

To find Italian-language newspapers that may have information on your ancestors, ask your elderly relatives if they remember the name of the paper they or their parents used to read. You may also check with the librarians in the communities where your ancestors lived. If your relatives lived in New York or New Jersey, you might look in issues of *Eco d'Italia* (Echo of Italy), published in New York City from 1849 to 1937, or *AVANTI! Giornale Socialista Italo-Americano*, published irregularly since 1904 in Newark, New Jersey.

Always remember that because something appears in print, it is not necessarily true. Suppose you find an old newspaper article stating that your great-grandfather died when he was sixty-nine. If you always cite your sources, you will be able to judge which source is more reliable in case of conflicting information. For example, if you later find a death certificate or last will and testament for your great-grandfather that shows he died at ninety-six, you can conclude that the typesetter at the newspaper made a mistake.

Source citations should include the author, name of the newspaper, date of publication, and name of the library where you found the information.

The National Archives

An archive is simply a place where official records are kept. Each state has a state archive, but you will probably find the National Archives more useful in your genealogical research.

The National Archives in Washington, DC, keep millions of records on the dealings anyone has had with the federal government. The most useful records for family historians are the census records, naturalization records, and customs and passenger lists for steamships carrying immigrants. The main address of the National Archives and the addresses of its eleven Regional Archives are listed in the **Resources**.

• Census Records. A census is a periodic counting of the number of people living in a certain place. The very first census was taken by the ancient Romans, who wanted to know how many citizens lived in Rome. While it would be fascinating to know if one of your ancestors lived in Rome over two thousand years ago, you should follow the general rule of genealogical research: Start with the most recent census records available and work backward in time.

From your interviews with relatives and others, you probably have a good idea of where the various family groups lived in, say, 1910. For example, if your grandmother was born in 1930 and you know the names of her parents and have a general idea where the family lived, you can probably find information on the family in the 1910 census. Depending on the year the census was taken, you'll find different information recorded.

This is some of the information you can learn from the census:

• Your ancestors' full names
• Who lived in your ancestors' households
• You ancestors' occupations at the time of the census
• Where your ancestors lived at the time of the census
• When ancestors were born or died

Since 1790, the United States government has held a census every ten years. The National Archives have microfilm of the 1880 census, fragments of the 1890 census, and the 1900 and 1910 censuses. These cover the great wave of Italian immigration, so it is very likely that your original Italian immigrant ancestors will be on one of these schedules. To order a copy from the National Archives, you need to know the census in which the person's name appears as well as the exact page number on which it appears. You can get this information from the indexes to the census schedules. Indexes are published by many private companies and individuals, and they can be found in most libraries and at the National Archives offices.

If there is no library or archive with census indexes near you, you may borrow census microfilm from The Church of Jesus Christ of Latter-day Saints Family History Centers, or from the American Genealogical Lending Library. More information on these organizations is given later in this chapter.

• Military Records. The National Archives is the largest repository of military records in the United States. Military service results in service records and benefits records. Finding an ancestor's military record will add to your family history in two ways. First, it is often a good way to locate male ancestors if you have no record of them in deeds, wills, or census records. Second, they can fill in what people were doing in their young adulthood, and their military achievements might add to the interest of your family history. Following the pattern of working from known information to unknown, begin by identifying family members who you know or think may have fought in United States wars. These wars include:

- The American Revolution (1776–1783)
- The War of 1812
- Wars with various Native American peoples in the early nineteenth century
- The Mexican-American War (1846–1848)
- The Civil War (1861–1865)
- The Spanish-American War (1898)
- World War I (1917–1918)

- World War II (1941–1945)
- The Korean War (1951–1953)
- The Vietnam War (1965–1975)
- The Gulf War (1992)

You may know which relatives fought in which wars from your interviews or from your research into census and county courthouse records. Pension records are especially useful in finding out if someone served in the military, since the federal government gives financial assistance to people disabled in military service and to the dependents of those killed in action.

Records for World Wars I and II, the Korean War, the Vietnam War, and the Gulf War are restricted under privacy laws. Contact the National Personnel Records Center, 9700 Page Boulevard, St. Louis, MO 63132, for additional information about service records for these wars.

For information on how to obtain military records about relatives who participated in the other wars, the National Archives publish a very helpful booklet, *Military Service Records in the National Archives.*

- Ships' Passenger Lists. The National Archives have partial customs passenger lists and immigration passenger lists dating back to 1820. The lists generally give the name of the ship, the ship's master, the port of embarkation in Italy, the date and port of arrival in the United States, and the name, age, sex, and occupation of each passenger. This data can be invaluable in your search for information about your original immigrant ancestors.

Name indexes are available in a number of publications (see **Resources** at the end of this chapter). You can use the index to look up your immigrant ancestor's name, port of entry, and date of arrival. With this information, you can then file a request for information with the National Archives. Use Form NATF 81, "Order of Copies of Passenger Arrival Records" to request a copy of the ship's passenger list on which your immigrant ancestor's name appeared.

- Naturalization Records. If you have enough information

about an immigrant's arrival, the Immigration and Naturalization Service (INS) can search its Alien Registration Records and Naturalization Records and send copies of pertinent records to you. These records give an immigrant's birthdate, age upon arrival, destination in the United States, and other information. To request a search for information from the INS, a branch of the Department of Justice, you have to fill out Form G-641, "Application for Verification from Immigration and Naturalization Records," and pay a fee. The forms are available at INS offices in major cities. Look in your phone book for an INS office in your city, or call the Washington, DC, office at 202-514-2000 for the address and phone number of the nearest office. For more information about how naturalization records can help in your genealogical research, see the **Resources**.

• Other National Archives Resources. The National Archives have many other potential resources for genealogists, including pamphlets and workshops. For information about what is available, write to: Reference Services Branch, The National Archives, Washington, DC 20408, or call 202-501-5400. To order publications or microfilm, call, write, or fax the Publications Services Staff (NEPS), Marketing and Fulfillment Branch, National Archives, Washington, DC 20408; 202-501-5240; Fax: 202-501-5239. You may also call or write the National Archives Regional Branch that serves your home state. See **Resources** for addresses.

The National Archives is only one of the many public and private organizations that publish pamphlets and guides to genealogical research and hold workshops for genealogists. Because hundreds of thousands of people are engaged in researching their family histories, a small support industry of magazines, publishing houses, and societies has sprung up. The **Resources** section lists many of these organizations.

The Library of The Church of Jesus Christ of Latter-day Saints

No discussion of genealogical research would be complete without mentioning the largest genealogical association and

library in the world: the Family History Library of The
Church of Jesus Christ of Latter-day Saints (LDS). Their
buildings in Salt Lake City house information on about 2
billion people. Although the library has been put together by
people of a particular faith, it contains information on families of many religious beliefs or places of origin. This information includes census records, church records, court
records, land grants, deeds, naturalization records, passenger
ship lists, marriage records, wills, and more.

The LDS library is well worth a trip if you live anywhere
near it. If you live far from Utah, you can still have access to
the resources of the library through its many research
centers. To find the LDS Family History Center nearest you,
look in your phone book, or write to the main LDS library at
35 North West Temple Street, Salt Lake City, UT 84150.

Other Genealogical Societies

The **Resources** section gives the names and addresses of the
major American genealogical societies. There is usually a
membership fee to join these organizations, but this fee is
often used to provide you with useful magazines and other
information. You can request the society's catalog of publications whether you decide to join or not.

Most public libraries subscribe to some genealogical periodicals, such as the popular *Everton's Genealogical Helper*.
Ask your local librarian for a few back issues. In this and
other publications, you'll often find classified ads in which
researchers ask for information on a particular surname,
army regiment, or graveyard that may lead to information
they need. As you skim through these ads, you may find
someone with information that will help you. Eventually you
may have gathered some information that can help others.
You'll find that the genealogical community is helpful and
open, always happy to welcome a new researcher.

Resources

VITAL RECORDS

Bureau of the Census
Pittsburg, KS 66762

Write to this address for information on censuses not yet made public. Ask for an order form and list of fees.

Civilian Personnel Records
111 Winnebago Street
St. Louis, MO 63118

Write and ask for an order form and information on civilian employees of the U.S. Government after 1909.

Dollarhide, William, and Thorndale, William. *Map Guide to the U.S. Federal Censuses, 1790–1920.* **Baltimore: Genealogical Publishing, 1987.**

A useful guide that shows which areas were covered in which censuses.

International Vital Records Handbook. **Baltimore: Genealogical Publishing Co., 1990.**

A collection of vital records application forms from around the world.

Kirkham, E. Kay. *A Handy Guide to Record-Searching in the Larger Cities of the United States.* **Logan, UT: Everton Publishers, 1974.**

A guide to vital records of cities, including street maps and indexes, and other information that can help you trace the life history of an ancestor.

Military Personnel Records
9700 Page Boulevard
St. Louis, MO 62132

Ask for Standard Form 180, "Request Pertaining to Military Records" for information on Army after 1912 or Marines after 1895.

Passport Office
State Department
Washington, DC 20520

Write here for passport applications after 1926.

Social Security Administration Death Master File.

This record of recently deceased Americans is available in microform from LDS Family History Centers. It includes names, date of death, place of death, and place of burial.

Where to Write for Vital Records: Births, Deaths, Marriages and Divorces.

You can order this booklet from the U.S. Government Printing Office, Superintendent of Documents, Washington, DC 20402. You may also request a brochure of publications relating to family research.

LIBRARIES

Anderson, Alloa Caviness. *Genealogical Research in Libraries.* **Ann Arbor, MI: Author, 1978.**

A good starting place for information on some of the useful genealogical resources in libraries.

Balhuizen, Anne Ross. *Searching on Location: Planning a Research Trip.* **Salt Lake City, UT: Ancestry, Incorporated, 1992.**

How to do the groundwork and organization that will make your library trips more productive.

Gilmer, Lois C. *Genealogical Research and Resources: A Guide for Library Use.* **Chicago: American Library Association, 1988.**

A good introduction to the resources available to genealogists.

Greenwood, Val D. *The Researcher's Guide to American Genealogy.* **Baltimore: Genealogical Publishing Co., 1990.**

A guide with tips on tracking down obscure sources of information.

Kaminkow, Marion J. *Genealogies in the Library of Congress: A Bibliography.* **Baltimore: Magna Carta, 1972.**

A very useful introduction to the family histories available in the Library of Congress.

————. *A Complement to Genealogies in the Library of Congress.* **Baltimore: Magna Carta, 1981.**

An essential update to the Library of Congress's collection.

McNeil, Barbara. *Biography and Genealogy Master Index, 1994.* **Detroit: Gale Research, 1993.**

This up-to-date index of biographies and genealogical sources is an invaluable guide to any family historian.

Moody, Suzanna, and Wurl, Joel, comps. and eds. *The Immigration History Research Center: A Guide to Collections.* **Westport, CT: Greenwood Press, 1991.**

Contains a description of the Italian American collection, approximately fourteen hundred items, including the archives of the Order of the Sons of Italy in America.

National Union Catalog of Manuscript Collections. **Washington, DC: Library of Congress, 1962.**

This catalog will guide you to manuscripts such as unpublished family histories.

Parker, J. Carlyle. *Going to Salt Lake City to Do Family History Research.* **Turlock, CA: Marietta Publishing, 1989.**

This book prepares you for a visit to the immense Family History Library. It offers advice on organizing and focusing your search before your visit.

———. *Library Service for Genealogists.* **Detroit: Gale Research Co., 1981.**

Information on where special collections and other resources can be found.

Russo, Pietro. *Italian-American Periodical Press, 1836–1980: A Comprehensive Bibliography.* **Staten Island, NY: Center for Migration Studies, 1984.**

Index to the Italian immigrant press. If your relatives lived in an urban Italian American community, there was probably a newspaper covering that community.

Stewart, J. *Discover Your American Heritage.* **Evans, GA: Ancestral Historical Society, 1981.**

Gives advice about obtaining assistance from U.S. Government records offices.

PASSENGER LISTS AND NATURALIZATION RECORDS

Cassady, Michael. *New York Passenger Arrivals, 1849–1868.* **Papillon, NE: S. Nimmo, 1983.**

Transcription of passenger lists found on microfilm copies at the National Archives.

Coletta, John P. *They Came in Ships: Finding Your Immigrant Ancestor's Arrival Record,* **2nd ed. Salt Lake City: Ancestry, Incorporated, 1993.**

A comprehensive manual, with extensive bibliography.

Filby, P. William, and Meyer, Mary K., compilers. *Passenger and Immigration Lists Index.* **Detroit: Gale Research Co., 1981.**

A three-volume index to published arrival records of about five hundred thousand passengers who came to the United States and Canada in the seventeenth, eighteenth, and nineteenth centuries. Annual supplements have been issued since 1982, each containing an additional 125,000 names.

Immigration and Naturalization Service Washington, DC 20536

Write for an order form for naturalization records after 1906.

Lancour, Harold, compiler. *A Bibliography of Ship Passenger Lists, 1538–1835.* **New York: New York Public Library, 1963.**

A useful list for finding pre-1835 immigrants.

Morton Allan Directory of European Passenger Steamship Arrivals for the Years 1890 to 1930 at the Port of New York and for the Years 1904–1926 at the Ports of New York, Philadelphia, Boston, and Baltimore. **New York: Immigration Information Bureau, Inc., 1931. Reprint, Baltimore: Genealogical Publishing Co., 1979.**

This work lists the arrivals of passenger steamships by calendar year and is indexed alphabetically by steamship line.

Neagles, James C., and Lee, Lila. *Locating Your Immigrant Ancestor: A Guide to Naturalization Records.* **Logan, UT: Everton Publishers, 1986.**

This book features an index of immigration records, listed

by state and county, dating back to 1837. It also describes the immigration process and the history of immigration patterns in the United States.

Tepper, Michael. *Passenger Arrivals at the Port of Philadelphia, 1800–1819.* **Baltimore: Genealogical Publishing Co., 1986.**

A transcription of baggage lists of about forty thousand immigrants who landed in Philadelphia. Historical background is provided in the introduction.

THE NATIONAL ARCHIVES

For general information and queries, write or call:
Reference Services Branch (NNRS)
National Archives
Washington, DC 20408
202-501-5400

To order publication or microfilm, call, write, or fax:
Publications Services Staff (NEPS)
Marketing and Fulfillment Branch
National Archives
Washington, DC 20408
202-501-5240
Fax: 202-501-5239

Guide to Genealogical Research in the National Archives. **Revised. Washington, DC: The National Archives, 1985.**

A guide to the records housed in the National Archives. Chapter 2 includes sections on passenger arrival lists, special notes by port of entry, and so on. The book also explains how to locate records and request copies.

You may also contact the regional branch of the National Archives that serves your area.

REGIONAL BRANCHES OF
THE NATIONAL ARCHIVES

Central Plans Region
2312 East Bannister Road
Kansas City, MO 64131
816-926-6272

Serving Iowa, Kansas, Missouri, and Nebraska.

Great Lakes Region
7358 South Pulaski Road
Chicago, IL 60629
312-581-7816

Serving Illinois, Indiana, Michigan, Minnesota, Ohio, and Wisconsin.

Mid-Atlantic Region
Ninth and Market Streets
Philadelphia, PA 19107
215-597-3000

Serving Delaware, Pennsylvania, Maryland, Virginia, and West Virginia.

New England Region
380 Trapelo Road
Waltham, MA 02154
617-647-8100

Serving Connecticut, Maine, Massachusetts, New Hampshire, Rhode Island, and Vermont.

Northeast Region
Building 22-MOTBY
Bayonne, NJ 07002
201-823-7241

Serving New Jersey, New York, Puerto Rico, and the Virgin Islands.

Pacific Northwest Region
6125 Sand Point Way, NE
Seattle, WA 98115
206-526-6507

Serving Alaska, Idaho, Oregon, and Washington.

Pacific Sierra Region
1000 Commodore Drive
San Bruno, CA 94066
415-876-9009

Serving Hawaii, Nevada except for Clark County, and northern California.

Pacific Southwest Region
P.O. Box 6719
Laguna Niguel, CA 92607-6719
714-643-4241

Serving Arizona, southern California, and Clark County, Nevada.

Rocky Mountain Region
Building 48
Denver Federal Center
Denver, CO 80225
or
P.O. Box 25307
Denver, CO 80225
303-236-0818

Serving Colorado, Montana, North Dakota, South Dakota, Utah, and Wyoming.

Southeast Region
1557 St. Joseph Avenue
East Point, GA 30344
404-763-7474

Serving Alabama, Florida, Georgia, Kentucky, Mississippi, North Carolina, South Carolina, and Tennessee.

Southwest Region
501 West Felix Street
Fort Worth, TX 76115
817-334-5525

Serving Arkansas, Louisiana, New Mexico, Oklahoma, and Texas.

GENEALOGICAL SOCIETIES AND PUBLICATIONS

American Genealogical Lending Library
593 West Street
P.O. Box 329
Bountiful, UT 84011

The AGLL rents microforms of indexes (vital records, censuses, etc.) for a reasonable fee. Ask your local librarian if they participate in AGLL programs. Soon these indexes will be out on CD-ROM.

Board of Certification of Genealogists
P.O. Box 5816
Falmouth, VA 22403-5816

For a current list of certified family history researchers, send a self-addressed, stamped envelope and $3.00 to this organization.

***Heritage Quest*. American Genealogical Lending Library.**

This bimonthly magazine has classified ads offering and seeking information and features columns on computer technology and adoption searches.

Meyer, Mary K. *Meyer's Directory of Genealogical Societies in the USA and Canada*. Mt. Airy, MD: Mary K. Meyer, 1988.

This book should be in your local library. Look at it to find societies in your region, societies that focus on Italian

American heritage, and societies that publish catalogs and manuals.

National Genealogical Society
4527 17th Street North
Arlington, VA 22207-2363

One of the largest family research associations, the NGS publishes and sells books, forms, and indexes. If you become a member, you will receive the *NGS Quarterly* and *NGS Newsletter*.

National Institute on Genealogical Research
P.O. Box 14274
Washington, DC 20044-4272

Gives workshops and publishes information.

POINTers
Box 2977
Palos Verdes, CA 90274

Quarterly journal of POINT (Pursuing Our Italian Names Together).

Schreiner-Yantis, Netti, ed. *Genealogical and Local History Books in Print*, 4th ed. 3 vols. Springfield, VA: 1990.

Catalogs hard-to-find manuscripts related to family research and lists vendors who sell genealogical publications, supplies, and services.

Chapter 6
Research in Italy

Most genealogists looking for their Italian roots trace their first immigrant ancestor to someone who came over during the great migration of 1890–1920. Only a few discover that their immigrant ancestor was one of the sculptors, winemakers, or other artisans who came to the United States in the seventeenth or eighteenth centuries.

The **Resources** on Censuses and Ships' Passenger Lists at the end of the preceding chapter provided several valuable references. The 1900, 1910, and 1920 censuses can be very helpful because they give a date of immigration for residents born overseas and indicate whether or not the resident has been naturalized. Federal censuses are available at the National Archives in Washington, DC, the twelve Regional Archives of the National Archives (see **Resources** at the end of Chapter 5 for addresses), and many libraries, including the LDS Family History Library in Salt Lake City.

Ships' passenger lists containing a variety of information can be found for all major U.S. ports of entry: New York, Boston, Philadelphia, Baltimore, and New Orleans. Before 1906, ships' passenger lists indicate only the nationality or country of origin or last permanent residence of the passenger. But beginning in 1906, they provide the town of birth. This is one of the important pieces of information you need to carry your genealogical search back to the "old country."

To research further back to the generations of your family in Italy, you must know a person's original name, approximate date of birth, and town of birth. The name is not always as easy as it might seem. Many Italian surnames were shortened or otherwise transformed when immigrants first came to the United States. The reasons for the changes and the family stories about surname changes are often interesting and amusing. You may want to include such stories in your final family history. To pursue your genealogical research in Italian records, you must be sure of your immigrant ancestor's original surname and given names.

The person's date of birth is also important because many Italian children had the same or similar names as their parents or other relatives. Knowing the birthdate will help you track down your immigrant ancestor—not his father, cousin, or uncle.

The person's town of birth is important to know because most civil and religious records in Italy are kept on the local level.

You may use many of the research techniques and sources already mentioned to gather these three facts. Start by reviewing your notes from oral interviews. You may have to go back to some of your elderly relatives and ask if they have old passports, letters, photographs, military discharge papers, citizenship certificates, steamship ticket stubs, or postcards showing the town of origin of the ancestor who first came to the United States.

When you know your immigrant ancestor's name and the date and place of birth, you may want to go to Italy someday and continue your research. Since there has been little centralization of records in Italy, you will probably need to go to your ancestor's hometown. There you'll see the hills and coasts your ancestors saw, sit in the same town squares, walk the same roads.

If you don't speak Italian, you should study a little before you travel. Even a smattering will help immensely. You'll also find Italian to be a language full of life and vigor. If you continue to study it, you may eventually read the beautiful words of Dante and other Italian writers in the original. Such an experience will also give you a feel for the language and the sensibility of your ancestors who emigrated from Italy.

On a more practical level, a little polite Italian will go a long way in getting church and civic officials to help you in

Travel to Italy will allow you to explore your family history and learn about Italian history and culture. It can be especially interesting to learn about the specific region from which your ancestors emigrated. Above, a woman poses for a portrait in traditional dress from the region of Sardinia, located off Italy's western coast.

your research. In your ancestor's hometown, or *frazoni*, you'll go to the town hall to find the civil registers. These registers contain the basic vital statistics of the residents of the town throughout the years. You may also find an *Anagrafe*, which is like a town census. The earliest ones date from approximately 1885.

Wills filed within the last century may be available from a local notary. The notary of the town today might be a great-great-grandson or nephew or cousin of the notary who lived when your ancestors were citizens of the town. In his records will be wills and other notarized papers from the last one hundred years or so. For wills older than one hundred years, write for information to Archivio Notarile Ispettatore Generale, Via Flaminia, 160, Rome, Italy.

Church records in Italy provide the same kinds of information as those in the United States—birth, baptism, first communion, marriage, and death. Go to the priests of local churches in your ancestor's hometown, explain that you are researching your family history, and ask if you might see the church records. Generally the priests are helpful, but unfortunately older church records have often been lost or destroyed. If they do exist, they are often damaged.

Even if the church records are damaged, they may be of more help than the emigration records. There are few such records in Italy because, especially before World War I, emigration was often a clandestine activity.

After exhausting the sources available in your ancestor's hometown, you might contact the official state archive of the province where your ancestor was born. There are nine of these state archives (*Archivio di Stato*): in Rome, Naples, Palermo, Venice, Turin, Milan, Genoa, Florence, and Bologna. The archives may contain records of genealogical interest. Especially useful are the *Leva*, or military conscription rolls of the nineteenth century.

Before going to Italy, be sure to do as much research as you can in the United States—the kind of research outlined in Chapters 3, 4, and 5. This research—interviews with relatives, visits to libraries, courthouses, and church archives, and accessing information from the National Archives, will form the basis of the research you do in Italy. Your U.S.-based research should be as complete and accurate as possible so that your time in Italy is well spent. Before making your travel plans, you should also call, write, or visit organizations that specialize in Italian American history and heritage. You may find them listed in your local phone book or that of a large town nearby. Often large universities have special collections devoted to Italian Americans. If you live near New York or Chicago, you might begin by contacting the Center for Migration Studies, Staten Island, New York, or the Italian American Collection, Special Collections, The University Library, The University of Illinois at Chicago.

Resources

Caroli, Betty Boyd. *Italian Repatriation from the United States, 1900–1914.* **New York: Center for Migration Studies, 1973.**

This book discusses the phenomenon of repatriation— Italians who lived and worked in the United States but eventually returned to Italy.

Cole, Trafford R. "Italian Genealogical Record Sources." *The Genealogical Helper,* **Vol. 34, Sept.– Oct., 1980, pp. 9–13.**

Good article with sample letters and photographs of three examples of Italian church records.

Guelfi Camajani, Guelfo. *Genealogy in Italy.* **Firenze: Instituto Genealogico Italiano, 1979.**

Brief, general overview (in English) of Italian archival resources.

Higdon, Rose Musacchio, and Higdon, Hal. *Falconara: A Family Odyssey.* **Michigan City, IN: Road Runner Press, 1993.**

The story of the authors' search for their family roots.

Preece, Floren Stocks, and Preece, Phyllis Pastore. *Handy Guide to Italian Genealogical Records.* **Logan, UT: Everton Publishers, Inc., 1978.**

Brief work providing some valuable information and research tips.

Records of Genealogical Value for Italy. **Salt Lake City, UT: Genealogical Department of The Church of Jesus Christ of Latter-day Saints, 1979. Series G, no. 2.**

For all major genealogical sources in Italy, this slim volume lists the types of records in existence, the time periods they cover, the information they contain, and their availability for searching.

RESEARCH AIDS

Andreozzi, John. *Guide to the Records of the Order of the Sons of Italy in America.* **St. Paul, MN: Immigration History Research Center, 1988.**

Describes the Order of the Sons of Italy in America archives, part of the Italian American collection in the Immigration History Research Center.

Carmack, Sharon DeBartolo. "Using Social Security Records to Test an Italian-American Family Tradition." *National Genealogical Society Quarterly***, Vol. 77, No. 4, December, 1989, pp. 257–259.**

Demonstrates how Social Security records may be obtained and used to resolve a genealogical problem.

———. "The Genealogical Use of Social History: An Italian-American Example." *National Genealogical Society Quarterly***, Vol. 79, No. 4, December, 1991, pp. 284–288.**

Illustrates the importance of learning local history to understand ancestors' lives and motivations.

Coletta, John P. "The Italian Mayflowers." *Attenzione***, February, 1984, pp. 30–33.**

Explains how to search the ships' passengers lists at the National Archives for Italian immigrants.

Fucilla, Joseph Guerin. *Our Italian Surnames.* **Baltimore: Genealogical Publishing, 1987.**

Gives the meaning of Italian surnames and which surnames are associated with which regions of Italy.

Lewanski, Rodolf J., comp. *Guide to Italian Libraries and Archives.* **New York: Council for European Studies, 1979.**

Describes the organization of Italian libaries and archives and gives a statistical profile of the major institutions.

Stych, F. S. *How to Find Out about Italy.* **Oxford: Pergamon Press, 1970.**

A guide to locating bibliographies and collections of works dealing with all aspects of Italian life and culture, including philosophy, religion, language, social sciences, literature, genealogy, heraldry, and more.

MANUALS FOR ITALIAN GENEALOGY

Baxter, Angus. *In Search of Your European Roots: A Complete Guide to Tracing Your Ancestors in Every Country in Europe.* **Baltimore: Genealogical Publishing, 1985.**

A thorough and reliable book that discusses Italian genealogy on pages 165–174.

Beard, Timothy Field, and Demong, Denise. *How to Find Your Family Roots.* **New York: McGraw Hill, 1977.**

Provides a thumbnail history of Italy and addresses of Italian archives and organizations.

Colletta, John Philip. *Finding Italian Roots: The Complete Guide for Americans.* **Baltimore: Genealogical Publishing, 1994.**

This guide explains how to find information about your ancestors who lived in Italy.

Glynn, Joseph Martin. *Manual for Italian Genealogy.* **Newton, MA: The Italian Family History Society, 1981.**

Most valuable for its lists of names and addresses of Italian and American societies, genealogists, archives, and libraries.

Italian Genealogist. **Torrance, California, Augustan Society.**

Periodical with articles and tips for researchers.

Konrad, J. *Italian Family Research*. **Munroe Falls, OH: Summit Publications, 1980.**

Addresses for conducting research in both the United States and Italy.

Robichaux, Albert J. *Italian-American Roots: The Civil Registration of Births, Marriages, and Deaths.* **Rayne, LA: Hebert Publishing, 1994.**

Deals with information to be found in the town of Alia in Sicily.

Chapter 7
Nontraditional Families

Genealogy does not discriminate. You don't need a drop of Italian blood to research the background of a famous Italian American or one of your adoptive family members. You do, however, need to be aware of every person's right to privacy. Never pry into an area that someone seems reluctant to talk about. Everyone has a legal right to privacy.

If you live in a family with only one parent, a grandparent, or other relatives, you can start your research with them. You need not know the name of both of your birth parents to engage in extensive genealogical research. You can use all the research techniques described in the preceding chapters to discover a great deal about the history of one side of your family.

If You Are Adopted

If you are adopted, first remember that a family is much more a bond of love than of biology. This bond may be stronger than your curiosity about your biological parents.

If you do want to look into your biological parents' family history, be forewarned that the process will be long and difficult. When a person is adopted, he or she receives a new birth certificate. In all states except Alabama, records of adoptions are sealed. This means that no one, even the adoptee, can ever look at them without court action. The law is meant to protect both you and your biological parents. People generally have very good reasons for making the difficult decision to put a child up for adoption. In most cases, it is best to keep the identity of birth parents a secret.

However, if you want to try to learn something about your biological parents, begin by asking your adoptive parents.

Chances are they know very little about your birth parents and where they live now, but perhaps they can tell you where you were born and how old you were when you were adopted.

After gaining as much information as you can from your adoptive parents, you can contact a number of national organizations that help adoptees search for their birth parents. The largest is the Adoptees Liberty Movement Association (ALMA), P.O. Box 154, Washington Bridge Station, New York, NY 10033; 212-581-1568. *People Searching News* is a newsletter for people searching for lost or missing family members. It has a hotline offering free assistance: 305-370-7100.

Writing Your Own History

Winston Churchill, a prime minister of Great Britain, once said, "History will be kind to me, for I intend to write it." You too can write history. The next chapter of this book focuses on writing your family history from the information you have gathered in interviews and other sources. There are other kinds of writing projects, too.

You can be the starting point of a family history of your own. One of the best ways to start is simply to keep a journal. Many people keep a notebook next to their beds and before going to sleep each night they write down some events and thoughts of that day. You may find it hard to start writing, but after a few sentences your thoughts will begin to flow and you may find it hard to stop. Do not worry about how interesting or "correct" your notes are— this is simply raw material.

Later, you can start organizing your journal entries into a more formal autobiography. The idea of telling your life story may seem scary at first. But you needn't start with your birth and describe each day after. Just start with any memory that comes to mind—about a place, an event, a person. Start with your earliest memories—include as many details as you can: What does your room, your house, your neighborhood look like? Who was your first friend? Who

taught you to ride a bicycle and to swim? Write down everything you can about your parents, teachers, classmates,
neighbors, siblings, and friends. You can embellish your
autobiography with your own sketches and photographs, or
with various memorabilia such as awards, diplomas, letters,
ticket stubs, and the like.

Your journal entries or autobiography give you a certain
kind of immortality—people born after you die will still be
able to know something about who you were and how you
lived. When you decide to finish your history, you can seal
the document in an envelope or box with directions on the
outside as to who should open it and when. Now you have
created a time capsule of information for your grandchildren
and great-grandchildren.

Resources

NONTRADITIONAL FAMILY HISTORY

Askin, Jayne, with Molly Davis. *Search: A Handbook for Adoptees and Birthparents.* **Phoenix: Oryx Press, 1992.**

A thorough guide to registers and searching aids.

Cohen, Shari. *Coping with Being Adopted.* **New York: Rosen Publishing Goup, 1988.**

A guide for teenagers who do not live with their biological parents. Includes a chapter on the pros and cons of searching for your birth parents.

Gouke, Mary Noel. *One-Parent Children, the Growing Minority.* **New York: Garland, 1990.**

A resource guide containing interviews with many children, teens, parents, and counselors. Includes suggestions on ways to cope with being the child of a single parent.

Krementz, Jill. *How It Feels to Be Adopted.* **New York: Knopf, 1982.**

In a series of interviews with child and adult adoptees, the author explores the special problems of adoptees, including curiosity about birth parents, social stigmas, and an unclear sense of self. The author herself is an adoptee.

Lifton, Betty Jean. *Lost and Found.* **New York: Perennial Library, 1988.**

The author, adopted and curious about her roots, begins searching for her heritage. This is the story of her journey to piece together her family tree.

People Searching News.

A magazine for adoptees and birth parents, published by J. E. Carlson and Associates, P.O. Box 22611, Ft. Lauderdale, FL 33335. 305-370-7100. Includes updates on adoptions, advocacy groups registries, and articles by adoptees and their experiences when seeking their heritage.

Witherspoon, Mary Ruth. "How to Conduct an Adoption Search." *Everton's Genealogical Helper*, **July/ August, 1994, p. 10.**

An essay on the difficulties and rewards of finding your biological heritage by an author who found over three hundred of her living blood relatives.

ADOPTION SUPPORT GROUPS

Adoptee's Liberty Movement Association (ALMA)
850 Seventh Avenue
New York, NY 10019

This is the best-known and most active group promoting adoptees' right to information about their birth parents. They have set up a Reunion Registry, which can be reached at 212-581-1568.

Adoptees and Birthparents in Search
P.O. Box 5551
West Columbia, SC 29171
803-796-4508

Adoptees' Rights Search
Xenia, OH 45385
419-855-8439

Adopted and Searching/Adoptee-Birthparent Reunion Registry
401 East 74th Street
New York, NY 10021
212-988-0110

Adoptees Together
Route 1, Box 30-B-5
Climax, NC 27233

Adoptive Families of America
3333 Highway 100 North
Minneapolis, MN 55422
800-372-3300 (24-hour hotline)

National Adoption Information Clearinghouse
11426 Rockville Pike
Rockville, MD 20852

Chapter 8
Putting It All Together

There is never a true end to genealogical research. If you wait to "finish" your research before writing up your family history and drawing your family tree, you may never do those two things. There will always be one more long-lost cousin to research, one more generation to go back.

Genealogical research may become a lifetime hobby for you, but at some point you will want to take a break and prepare a written history and a family tree. Don't worry about a few blank lines on your family group sheets and pedigree charts. There are bound to be some facts that resist even your best research efforts. As you know from your own life experience, it is never worthwhile to bang your head against a shut door.

Writing Your Family History

As you sit and stare at your pages of notes and files of documents, the idea of writing up a family history may seem overwhelming. But if you have an orderly file system, you are already halfway to a book about your family history. In fact, some people simply buy a new looseleaf notebook and arrange their files in the notebook, with dividers separating family groups.

There are as many kinds of family history reports as there are genealogists. You should choose a style and form that fit your talents. Some people prepare a video report; others a written report; others a family tree with illustrations and anecdotes. Most commonly, genealogists report the results of their research in a family history, a book that includes the names, dates, places, and other information they have uncovered. To prevent it from becoming a dry recitation, many people also include stories from the interviews they conducted, old photographs, and other memorabilia.

Here is a sample table of contents for a family history:

- Cover or frontispiece. This might be a drawing or photograph of your extended family, a portrait of an ancestor, an old homestead, or a map showing the travels of your immigrant ancestor and the places in the United States where his or her descendants are living today. Use your own creative talents.
- Title page. This should have your report's title, your name, and the date.
- Foreword, acknowledgments, and dedication. In these pages you may explain what you have written and why. You may include some unusual or amusing incidents that occurred while you were writing the history. You may also use this page to thank the people who helped you in your research. You may choose to dedicate your book to someone important to you.
- A short autobiographical essay. Tell the reader who you are and why you did this genealogical research.
- Chapters with family group sheets and pedigree charts. This section contains the results of your research and can be organized in many ways. It should cover the story of your pre-United States ancestry, your immigrant ancestor(s), and the family lineage of succeeding generations to the present.
- Photographs, family sayings, family recipes, other family traditions. These add colorful detail to historical facts.
- Index of names. An index allows family members and others to easily find information on certain people.

In writing up the bulk of your family history, first decide on a starting point. Perhaps you will want to write about all the descendants of a particular ancestor. Or you may describe your research and the information you uncovered in chronological order, starting with yourself and your immediate family and moving backward in time to the earliest generations you could find information on.

You may want to include copies of family group sheets and pedigree charts, as well as copies of original documents and old photographs. If you conducted oral history interviews, you can enliven your family history with some of the interviewees' stories and comments on the places and times they lived in.

After you have all your material together, decide how to present it. The easiest way is probably simply to place it in a three-ring binder. For more permanent binding, you can ask about the different types of binding and their costs at a local copy shop or print shop. The best may be velo-binding with acetate covers.

If you are especially happy with your final product, you may want to publish it. Subsidy publishers, or vanity presses, will produce a finished book from your manuscript and print as many copies as you are willing to pay for.

There are many subsidy publishers throughout the country. Look in the yellow pages of your local phone book under "Publishers." If there are none near you, write to Vantage Press, 516 West 34th Street, New York, NY 10001, or call 1-800-821-3990 for a free guidebook to self-publishing (brochure TD-2). Another publisher, Carlton Press, 11 West 32nd Street, Dept. NYE, New York, NY 10011, 212-714-0300, offers a guide, *How to Publish Your Book*, which you can also order by mail or telephone.

Before publishing your work, review all your source citations and be sure that the information is as accurate as possible. Your finished report should include the source citations. All interview transcripts should have the informant's name, date, and place. Photocopies should have the source written on the back. This source material will be extremely helpful to anyone who may want to continue your efforts.

Family Tree
A family tree is a visual map of the results of your research.

You can get preprinted blank family trees from genealogy supply companies and publishers, or you can draw your own. A family tree can be as small as a single sheet of notebook paper or as large as a wall chart. You will probably want to sketch out your family tree first. Go through your notes and make sure all your information is in the correct folders. Then sketch a family tree by transcribing names from each family folder onto a branch of the family tree.

Your family tree can have names only, but it will be more meaningful if you include the person's birthdate, birthplace, marriage date, death date, and burial place. If you come to a branch where information is missing, just leave blanks. You may also want to include photographs of as many relatives as possible.

As you write your family history and draw up your family tree, take a moment to step back and savor the fruits of your genealogical investigation. Through your research in attics and archives and through your interviews with relatives and neighbors, you've learned many things. Most likely, you've discovered a number of people who are a lot like you—full of hopes and dreams, plans and schemes. Like yours, their lives had moments of great happiness and excitement as well as moments of unhappiness and disappointment. Each time you discovered the answers to *who? when? where?* and *why?* you extended the knowledge of your family history further and further into the past. At the same time you extended your knowledge further and further inward—to the real center of your study—yourself.

Resources

WRITING YOUR FAMILY HISTORY

Barnes, Donald R. *Write It Right: A Manual for Writing Family Histories and Genealogies.* **Bowie, MD: Heritage Books, 1987.**

A step-by-step manual to writing your history.

Dixon, Janice T., and Flack, Dora D. *Preserving Your Past: A Painless Guide to Writing Your Autobiography and Family History.* **Garden City, NY: Doubleday, 1977.**

As the authors say, this is a painless, even fun guide to writing up your research.

Huberman, Bob. *Video Portraits: The User-Friendly Guide to Videotaping Your Family History, Stories, and Memories.* **Bowie, MD: Heritage Books, 1987.**

If you feel more comfortable behind a camera than with a pen and paper, read this book and think about doing your family history on videotape.

Shull, Wilma Sadler. *Photographing Your Heritage.* **Salt Lake City, UT: Ancestry Incorporated, 1989.**

This book tells how you can photograph relatives and artifacts to illustrate your family history.

Smith, Lorna Diane. *Genealogy Is More than Charts.* **Ellicott City, MD: LifeTimes, 1991.**

This book provides many hints and examples of ways to enhance your family history.

Whitaker, Beverly DeLong. *Beyond Pedigree: Organizing and Enhancing Your Work.* **Salt Lake City, UT: Ancestry Incorporated, 1993.**

> Your family history can be much more than filled-in charts. This book gives you some ideas on how to flesh it out.

Zinsser, William. *On Writing Well: An Informal Guide to Writing Nonfiction.* **New York: Harper and Row, 1985.**

> Last, but certainly not least, be sure to read this classic book on how to write nonfiction. It is clear and to-the-point and will help you write anything from a letter requesting information to your final family history.

SELF-PUBLISHING

Henderson, Bill, ed. *The Publish-It-Yourself Handbook.* **Yonkers, NY: Pushcart Book Press, 1973.**

> The original classic on self-publishing. Advice from more than two dozen veteran self-publishers.

Hofmann, William J. *Life Writing: A Guide to Family Journals and Personal Memoirs.* **New York: St. Martin's Press, 1982.**

> A very useful book for writing your own history.

Poynter, Dan. *The Self-Publishing Manual.* **Santa Barbara, CA: Parachuting Publications, 1979.**

> How to write, print, and sell your own book.

Glossary

Anagraphe   Registrar's office.

agrarian   Relating to farmers or land.

anarchist   A believer in the theory that all government is undesirable.

authoritarian   Characterized by the concentration of political power in an authority not responsible to the people.

birth parents   Biological parents of a child.

campanilismo   A strong feeling of loyalty to the community within earshot of one's local church tower, or *campanile*.

characteristic   A distinguishing trait or quality.

corroborate   To confirm or support with evidence.

deforestation   The process of clearing an area of forests.

émigré   Person who emigrates, often for political reasons.

feudal system   A medieval European political organization characterized by the rendering of service to a lord by a tenant, who received land and protection in return.

frazione   A village.

fresco   A painting done by the method of painting on fresh plaster.

genetic   Relating to heredity.

greenhorn   An inexperienced person, especially one who is easily cheated.

Mafia   Secret criminal society originating in Italy and Sicily.

Mezzogiorno   A term referring to the regions of southern Italy, Calabria, and Sicily.

millennia   Thousands of years.

missionary   Person commissioned by a church to promote its faith.

naturalization The process of conferring the rights of citizenship.

padroni Italian Americans who served as middlemen between employers and workers. The *padrone* often exploited workers while at the same time providing them with useful services.

papacy The office of pope.

patent A document securing to an inventor exclusive rights to an invention for a term of years.

pedigree chart Chart that shows family lines at a glance.

peninsula A long, narrow portion of land extending into the water.

permeate To seep through.

piecework Work paid for by the individual unit or piece.

quarantine Restrictions on the movement of persons to prevent the spread of infection or disease.

scapegoat One that bears the blame for others.

steerage The below-deck section of a steamship, for which the cheapest tickets were sold.

strike To stop work in order to improve conditions of employment.

temperance Moderation in or abstinence from the use of alcoholic beverages.

unification The act or process of becoming a coherent whole.

Index

ABOUT THE AUTHOR
Terra Castiglia Brockman is a writer and editor living in New York City. Her maternal grandparents emigrated from southern Italy in the early part of the twentieth century and settled in Chicago.

ILLUSTRATION CREDITS
Cover, © Mark Bolster/International Stock; cover inset, courtesy of the author. Pp. 5, 7, 19, 21, 24, 30, 32, 36, 39, 41, 45, 49, 54, 88, 93, 145, BETTMAN; pp. 2, 110, courtesy of the author. *Color insert*: pp. 2, 3, 4, 5, 6, 7, 8, 10, 11, 12, 15, 16, BETTMAN; pp. 9, 13, 14, © Ken Martin/ Impact Visuals.

LAYOUT AND DESIGN
Kim Sonsky